Dynamic Women®

CONFIDENCE
Secrets!

Top Thought Leaders, Experts & Dynamic Women®
Share their Stories &
Secrets on Confidence!

Featuring
Diane Rolston
and other Leading
Entrepreneurs & Professionals

DEDICATION

This book is dedicated to all the Dynamic Women®
out there and those who raised them:

*

The ones who go for it, even when others say they can't.

*

The ones who give a hand up when they are asked.

*

The ones who ask for help, guidance & whatever they need.

*

The ones who are fearless on the outside, yet fearful inside.

*

The ones who choose to change & those forced to change.

*

The ones who are awarded & those who silently excel.

*

The ones who lead the way & those who support them.

*

The ones who blaze a trail, speak up & don't take crap.

*

The ones who listen openly, cry hard, & love unconditionally.

*

The ones who know they're Dynamic
& those who don't realize it yet.

*

The ones who are Y

WHAT OTHERS ARE SAYING
ABOUT DIANE ROLSTON and THIS BOOK

"This is a wonderful book that shows you immediately how to be happier and fulfill your unlimited potential."
~ **Brian Tracy,** Speaker, Author, Consultant

"If you're ready to take your business and life to higher levels and sustain continuous growth and improvement, then you must work with my friend Diane. Here's the great thing about Diane - she focuses on getting you rapid results by getting you laser focused, cutting you through the clutter and inspiring you to produce outcomes! And, Diane comes from the heart and truly cares about making a positive difference in the lives of others! Do yourself a favor and work with Diane today! You'll be so grateful you did!"
~ **James Malinchak**, Featured on ABCs Hit TV Show, "Secret Millionaire", Keynote Speakers & Business Coach

"Our long-term goals for our audience were met and we received very positive feedback about the event including, "Empowering, Inspirational & Fun!" If the women in your community are ready to be recharged and inspired, I would recommend Diane Rolston for your next event."
~ **Mae Legg,** Senior Small Business Consultant
Brantford-Brant Business Resource Centre

"I have participated in Diane's Dynamic Women® groups over the last few years for continued personal and professional development. Diane's high energy and co-active coaching skills are utilized in this group setting as they are in her Dynamic Year program. I would highly recommend working with Diane on goal setting as she has the experience, an encouraging way, and cuts through to the crux of the matter."
~ **Kirsten Anderson**, Founder Integrate Play Solutions

"Diane Rolston is of the most engaging and positive speakers on leadership and success."

~ Kevin Harrington, Original Shark from Shark Tank, Inventor of the Infomercial

"Diane has been my coach and I have grown so much through my work with her. When I started, I was looking to launch my business and with her help, I launched. I really couldn't have got there without her help. Diane is a fabulous coach who lovingly challenges you to move towards your dream life. She is honest and direct with your best interests in mind. Her various programs (Dynamic You, Dynamic Year, Dynamic Balance, Dynamic Business Success Formula, and others) have all been extremely helpful in my growth both in business and in my personal life. Thanks Diane for all your help."

~ Brenda Benham, Presentation Specialist

"Diane provides you with a roadmap for achieving your goals!"

~ Joe Theismann, Legendary NFL World Champion Quarterback & Entrepreneur

"I have been working with Diane for a few years now both in Dynamic Women (her sharing sessions are legendary) and as a client. Her masterminds are simply amazing! This year I became an Elite Coaching Client and the result still amazes me - I've worked through skills, concepts, and so much more to develop my business model. She is incredibly patient, knowledgeable, helpful, professional, kind, genuine and really cares about the success of each of her clients. I cannot recommend Diane enough. I thank Diane for all that she has given me - support, an ear, expertise, plus much more as I navigate this new world of business. I highly recommend her."

~ Kathy Fester, Chief Gratitude Officer of K.I.T. (Keep in Touch) Communications

Motivate, Inspire & Empower Those Around You with the Confidence Secrets!

SHARE THIS BOOK WITH OTHERS

Retail $29.95

Special Quantity Discounts

5-20 Books	$21.95
21-99 Books	$18.95
100-499 Books	$15.95
500-999 Books	$10.95
1000+ Books	$8.95

To Place and Order Contact:

(778)235.5819
info@dianerolston.com
www.dianerolston.com

TABLE OF CONTENTS

ACKNOWLEDGMENTS

I'd like to acknowledge my Dynamic Women® Global Club Members who have believed in the vision and mission of Dynamic Women®. You have been the reality to my dream, the fuel to my fire, and the reason why I do what I do.

I'm acknowledging all of the authors: having so many of my Dynamic Women® members, clients and connections in this book has made it a complete joy to publish together. You are all wonderfully Dynamic Women!

Thanks to Kate Bailey, Paula Kent and my team for their support in bringing this book to life.

"Fill your cup
today to have
ENERGY tomorrow."

~ DIANE ROLSTON

A Welcome Message to You from Diane

Hello there lovely! I wanted to connect with you personally before you read this Book.

You have made a wise decision to read this book. It is the 2nd in the series of Dynamic Women® Secrets books, with *Dynamic Women® Success Secrets* being the 1st. Whether you are already very confident or feel like you need lots of growth in this area, you will learn, be inspired, and use the secrets to be more confident. You will love hearing from so many incredible women. Many of whom are clients, colleagues, and friends of mine. You'll even hear from my daughter who is nine. Everyone has their view on what it takes to be confident in a particular area of life, in a unique situation or a specific industry.

When I coach my clients, lead Dynamic Women® events and speak to audiences, I see that so many women wish things could be different—that they could be different. I hear women yearning for more confidence. It's not about being different; it's more about focusing on what skills to build and grow to master confidence. This message is why I wanted to put together a book to bring you the stories and secrets from women on confidence. Being confident is also one of the 9 Pillars of being a Dynamic Woman. My contribution to this book is from my Program and Book called *Dynamic You.*

I have found that not only do women want to be confident in every area of life and every situation. They also wish they could step out of the day-to-day and into what they truly want and feel more self-assured about it. They aspire to belong in every place and every situation. They wish obstacles felt easier and smaller. That their goals felt within reach, and they wish they had a reliable system to pursue these things so that nothing would get in their way. Do you feel any of this?

It is why *Dynamic You* came to be. I've pieced together my experience in leading over 400 workshops from years of coaching, facilitating countless Dynamic Women® events, and numerous speaking engagements. I have collected the knowledge I have acquired from all the women I've met through my events and international coaching clients. I have compiled every bit of invaluable information, piecing it together into an 8-week program. The same program through which I have trained hundreds of other women—and you will receive some of the information about the 8th Pillar in *Dynamic You* at the start of this book.

You have the opportunity to treat it like a training program and apply what I am teaching. While you don't have the other 8 Pillars, and I am not leading you through group coaching, you will still gain knowledge, understanding and tools to become more confident.

When I wondered what I should share as my contribution to the book, I kept returning to the 8th Pillar and what I teach in the program. The information in Dynamic You™ is the foundation on which I shifted my life. Since then, I've been living in brilliance and successfully realizing my goals. You can make the shift too! If you want to know more about the rest of the Pillars and the program, please go to www.dianerolston.com/dynamicyou.

Remember, the most successful and wealthiest people in the world read lots of books, so you are already on the right path. Now it is time to implement what you read about in the 32 secrets, my section and the bonus material that will help during this pandemic. *Dynamic Women® Confidence Secrets* holds the tools you need to enable a shift in your mindset. This shift will support your growth and ramp up what is possible, empowering you to achieve better results. I feel blessed that I get to impact others and inspire them, and I'm so grateful for every day that I get to continue to live this DYNAMIC life. And I'm thankful for people like you who choose to grow!

Stay Dynamic!

Diane

Diane Rolston
Award-Winning Coach,
Speaker, Author, Podcaster,
CEO & Founder of Dynamic Women®
Wife & Mom of two

P.S. Here are 3 FREE opportunities to learn, grow and connect with Diane:

1. Grab your Free Gift and Diane Rolston's Website:
www.dianerolston.com/freegift

2. Listen and be inspired on the Dynamic Women Podcast:
https://podcasts.apple.com/us/podcast/id1467049886

3. Join free trainings, & connect with other Dynamic Women® in the FREE Facebook group:
www.facebook.com/groups/DynamicWomenGlobalClub/

About the Publisher: Diane Rolston is a leading authority in being a Dynamic Woman® and living a Dynamic Life. Combining a mix of coaching and personal development, Diane works with women to provide clarity, boost confidence and get them into action. She is a Certified Professional Coach, an International Speaker, Author, Workshop Leader and the CEO and Founder of Dynamic Women® Global Club and Podcast a quickly expanding  community of women. She was acknowledged as the Women of Worth "Motherpreneur of the Year" Award Winner, Top Mom Blogger in Vancouver, and Top 50 Mom Podcaster for her professional accomplishments and for the powerful impact she has on the women she inspires and empowers.

Diane left the life of the 9-5 employee and simultaneously became an entrepreneur and mother. Now a mother of two, business owner and community leader she considers herself an expert in change, work/life balance, prioritizing and getting things done! Diane's diverse work experience enables her to have a deeper understanding of what it takes to achieve our best and to live with more confidence and satisfaction. She believes we are not defined by our titles and our roles, instead we are more powerful and happy when we can be who we are. This brought out "Dynamic You", a book and a program, where she leads women to unleash the Dynamic Woman in them.

With her special mix of dynamics and heart she founded the group called, Dynamic Women®, where she facilitates engaging activities called "Coaching in Action" to help women get clear about their greatness, their success catalysts and the solutions to the obstacles (and all the while building strong relationships with other dynamic women). They meet and connect at live in person and virtual events.

Diane has presented at international women's business seminars, professional development conferences, in house for companies and on summits. She can speak to groups ranging from 10-10,000+. With clients across North America she has worked with non-profit executives, top management leaders, small business owners, and professional women helping them get better results in a shorter amount of time. She sees women sabotage themselves, get overwhelmed and second-guess their choices and uses her powerful questions to give clarity to what they really want and how they are going to achieve it. In 1:1 coaching sessions or one of her programs like "Dynamic Balance", she helps people break down big goals and build confidence so they can tackle their greatest obstacles, fears and reach more success.

Diane is a behind the scenes business advisor and coach for many business professionals, speakers, authors, thought leaders, and high achievers. Teaching anyone who wants to increase their results, how to correctly manage, package, and sell their time, experience, and expertise. Clients tell Diane that they love her sense of humor. That, "She's a positive person who constantly challenges your limits and helps you keep growing". Audiences comment on her dynamic style and how she always gives them a tool or challenge they can put into action and inspires them to make the changes they have been putting off.

In her own pursuits she pushes her limits, faces what scares her and loves to tackle a variety of projects. As a mother, wife, coach and business owner Diane acts with love and courage because she knows that in all parts of our life, we have the opportunity to inspire others. More than anything, she focuses on her goals in life and helps other women do the same.

Get all set at www.dianerolston.com for more clarity, confidence and action in your life and business.

Diane is the ideal speaker for your next conference or event. Email info@dianerolston.com to share about your speaker needs.

To see her in action, go to:

www.dianerolston.com/speaking

Connect with Diane on LinkedIn:

www.linkedin.com/in/dianercoaching

Connect with Diane personally on Facebook:

www.facebook.com/dianerolstoncoach

Connect with Diane professionally on Facebook:

www.facebook.com/LifeCoachDiane

Learn from Diane on YouTube:

www.youtube.com/c/CoachDianeRolston

Connect with Diane Rolston on Twitter:

https://twitter.com/DianeRCoaching

Diane Rolston on Instagram:

www.instagram.com/coachdianerolston/

Dynamic Women® is an international community of success-oriented women who take action to develop skills, increase results and are focused on supporting each other to be DYNAMIC in every area of life! Our members get access to success coaching, additional online educational activities, and the invaluable networking connections they need to reach their personal or professional goals.

Go to www.dynamicwomenclub.com to learn more and join the Global Club.

Want to be an author in a Dynamic Women® Secrets Book? Learn more here: www.dianerolston.com/be-an-author.html

Be Confident
Pillar 8 from the Program & Book
"Dynamic You"
By Diane Rolston

Pillar Eight is all about being confident. Dynamic Women® are confident, and if they aren't at first, they fake it until they make it. You want to be in a place where you are confident in every area of your life and every situation. I know that's not going to be the case for a lot of us. I don't feel confident in every single moment, but what I'm going to give you right now are seven ways we kill and zap away our confidence. Then, I'm going to provide you with seven solutions for being more confident.

I want you to think right now. What is your initial reaction to the idea of being more confident? Some of the ladies in my program reacted this way:

"Awesome, this is so important!"

"At first, I thought Eek! But I know it's something to work on."

"It's always something you're striving for."

"There are many layers to confidence, and hearing you break them down will be really helpful."

You are often in stages of confidence in a specific role, such as in being a parent. You can start to be confident with your baby, and then she hits the terrible twos. It's a constant cycle of mastering where you are, being confident. And then you move into a new stage and start all over, feeling like you're a novice in your confidence.

I have some other questions for you:

1. Do you believe yourself to be a confident person?

It's a yes or no. Yes? No?

If you think that sometimes you feel confident and other times you don't, give yourself a score out of 100%.

2. What percentage of the time are you confident? I want you to share your answer on the Dynamic You™ Global Community. For example, I am confident 80% of the time or 25% of the time. Whatever your number is, please share it.

Being confident as a Dynamic Woman is so important that many of the 9 pillars won't work otherwise. For example, being Magnetic and having charisma requires confidence. We want to make sure that this Pillar is strong for you.

You might be thinking, "Oh, I'm not a confident person," but having confidence in yourself isn't necessarily something you're born with. Confidence is something that you can build. You can increase your confidence. It's just a state of mind, and if you work on the little tricks I give you, you too can grow a kind of confidence that will be evident in every situation. That's 100% of the time AND in every area of your life. Sound good?

What is crucial to do first is to stop comparing yourself to everyone else. I invite you to think of yourself and how awesome you are. You have achieved, you have grown, and you are doing great things in your life. So, we are not going to catch compare-itis. We are not going to suffer from comparing and judging and all the consequences that follow. I want us to be in this place of self-confidence.

Confidence, Not Ego
On the other end of the spectrum, I don't want us to have too much confidence, where it turns into arrogance or the ego taking control. In my Dynamic Power™ Program, I talk about Power Over and Power Under.

Power Over

Having too much confidence or Power is a problem because it can put you in a Power Over position. This position is where you will order people around, be a bully and take advantage of those not as strong as you.

Power Under

A lack of confidence puts you in a Power Under position. I want us to think about being in that Personal Power Sweet Spot™ and applying that logic to a 'Confidence Sweet Spot.' When I teach my clients what their Personal Power Sweet Spot™ is, they gain confidence in being in that place because they see the results.

I'm going to take you through ways of building your confidence, but not to the extreme of arrogance. We know that Dynamic Women® are not arrogant, and they do not allow their egos to run the show. They are both humble and confident. They stand firm in knowing who they are, what they can provide and offer. Dynamic Women® stand up for themselves.

7 Ways We Kill Our Own Confidence

1. Procrastination and Perfectionism

Killer of confidence number one is Procrastination and Perfectionism because these two evil "Ps" go hand in hand. Often, we procrastinate because we don't know how to do something because we are scared of doing something or don't want to do something. The other reason we procrastinate is that we think that whatever we do should be perfect. We want it to be perfect, and so we don't move forward out of fear of being less than ideal. When you are engaging in procrastination and focusing on perfectionism, you are actively destroying your confidence.

The Solutions to Procrastination and Perfectionism

I can offer a couple of solutions to procrastination and perfectionism. If you hang out with doers, those who don't procrastinate and people who don't suffer from perfectionism, their approach will rub off on you. You can talk to them. You can follow them. You can hang out with them. Being around them will give you the confidence to step forward to do things. Doing something means you are not procrastinating. You are going to use them as role models. You are going to ask them for advice. You can look up to them for inspiration. Keep them around you because they are a better role model for you than someone who always procrastinates or is a perfectionist.

Make sure in your circle that you include some people who show their confidence by stepping forward, even into things they don't know how to do. To overcome the tendency to strive for perfectionism, you need to start valuing less than perfect results.

I mentioned how perfectionists compare themselves to others. However, the problem becomes worse if they're merely beginners and compare themselves to those years ahead. It's an unfair benchmark, and you'll never match the expectation of being at a level you can't possibly achieve, given the lack of time and experience. However, if you feel like you need to compare yourself to others for research or assessment purposes, compare yourself with somebody who is at your same level, not someone who is further ahead, because all you're going to do is judge yourself.

Compare yourself to others only when it will support your growth by asking yourself,

What are my competitors doing well? Where can I improve, and how can I stand out?

What's that person doing that helps them succeed?

Or, I met this person who's working in the same position as me, how can I learn from what she is doing?

What are the people ahead of me doing? Do I like it?

And if yes, how can I bring that in over the next six months to a year?

Additionally, do something you've been procrastinating on. That's your homework. Is there something on your to-do list you have avoided for a long time? Do it, even if you don't possess all the tools, even if you don't know everything, just do it. If you need to know something in order to get it done, then figure it out, because a lot of the time, we procrastinate because we don't know what the next step is. Let me know on the Facebook Community the one thing you've been procrastinating that you will start and finish.

2. Overwhelm

Killer of confidence number two, you are overwhelmed. So many things in your life, so many things to do, your schedule is full. You have no time, and you have so many things going on, and everything is so big. Life is overwhelming. So, where do you even start? If you have been in that situation, you know how it can kill your confidence. When you're overwhelmed, you're not in your brilliance. Instead, you worry about getting things done, and you're in a place of lacking, not enough time, energy, money, or perhaps lacking something else.

The trouble is we expect so much of ourselves every moment of every day. We over-schedule, we don't make time for ourselves. We don't eat well; we don't exercise, relax or sleep enough. We run ourselves into the ground because the expectations we have of ourselves are so high. More often than not, it's a super long list that no one could ever get done, and then we have low expectations of ourselves long-term. Instead, we need to lower our daily expectations for ourselves and raise our lives' overall expectations.

Try this quick activity, list out the things you need to do today—next list out the things you need to before the end of your life.

If you stopped to do this activity, you would probably have the same result as my clients: When I ask people what their plan for the day is, and then the plan for their life, the day list is often longer. We often expect so much from ourselves in the short term and don't dream big enough for ourselves in the long term.

The Solutions to the 'Overwhelm'

Instead of being in that overwhelming place, you need to create a plan, a plan that has a step-by-step guide illustrating what you're going to do to get moving. The trouble with our calendar is that we schedule projects rather than tasks. To not be overwhelmed, all you need to do is take the first step. You don't need to worry about 20 steps from now. Take the first step, complete a small task. It will build your confidence so that you can say to yourself, "Okay, I'm not overwhelmed by focusing on all the things I must do. Instead, I'm focusing on only the next step and the next step and then the next step. I can do it!" Soon, if you learn to work like this all the time, every time you make one of those small steps, you build trust in yourself, trust that you can make big goals happen. Big things happen in my life just by taking it all one step at a time. Completing small tasks and small things every day will add up to significant results.

Another solution you can do is set a small goal and achieve it. Rather than focusing on merely small tasks, break a large goal into smaller goals. If you select a goal of losing 20 pounds, why don't you start with a goal of losing one? If you set the goal of being healthier, why don't you just focus on drinking eight glasses of water a day first? Set that as your goal. Put a small achievable goal in place. You don't have to take everything on at one time. You don't have to take on the world on day one.

Some questions to check in with yourself are:

- Am I realistic with what I want to accomplish today?
- What are my top three priorities of what I need to accomplish?
- What structures need to be in place so I can do them?
- How am I going to celebrate after I accomplish them?
- What structures need to be in place next time to do this better?

If you want to boost your confidence, choose something you know you can and will achieve. I remember working with a client who kept making these outrageous goals. Each goal was more complicated than the last, and she set too many of them. She felt defeated by the end of the year because she didn't achieve many of her goals. Of course, she didn't because other unique opportunities arose, and she ended up wanting to do other things. She didn't re-evaluate her goals, and she still kept them big and out of reach. At the end of the year, she thought, "I'm a loser. I didn't do all these things". If she had just been a little more realistic in what she wanted to accomplish and acknowledged her achievements, she would have been in a better place.

You can also give yourself time after you complete a task to let your mind wander. This helps you to process what you went through and be more productive in moving forward. When people pack their day with no downtime, the mind waits for some quiet time to process everything. If the mind doesn't get this time to reflect, it will often choose some of the worst times to process things. For example, when you need to focus on an important task, when you're trying to relax at the spa, or when you're in your bed at night and trying to fall asleep.

The final solution to not being overwhelmed is to change one small habit. Maybe you can just go to bed earlier. Perhaps you can wake up earlier. How about you journal or write down five points of gratitude, stop smoking, or stop eating so much sugar. Just tell yourself, "I am going to do this one little thing. Just one little thing for 30 days." And stick to that. That is going to boost your confidence. The more you commit to something, follow through and do it, the more you will trust yourself to make even more goals and follow through with them as well.

3. Negative Self-Talk

Killer of confidence number three is negative self-talk and also negative thoughts. These thoughts can arise when you try new things or go for your goals, and for some, it's every waking moment.

The Solution to Negative Self-Talk

The solution is getting to know yourself. When you get to know yourself and listen to your thoughts rather than smother them, you stop worrying. You start processing. A client of mine experienced this the other day. She is just so busy. She doesn't make time in her day to process what she is going through, so if she wakes up in the middle of the night, she can't get back to sleep because she's worrying.

Another client of mine says she can't even get to sleep at night because her mind wanders. If she just acknowledged her thoughts at the moment throughout her day, her mind wouldn't need to try to process things at night when she should be sleeping. To get to know yourself profoundly, your inner dialogue would sound something like this: "Interesting. I react this way in this situation," or "I don't like that I did this," or "I don't possess these skills." The more you can make your self-observations factual, rather than emotionally based judgements, the more you remove negative self-talk and start to think and act positively.

Maybe you have heard before how thinking positively changes you because your beliefs become your thoughts, which become your words, which become your actions and then others' reactions. I not only want you to be thinking positively but also acting positively. What does that look like for you?

The final solution for negative self-talk is to focus on precisely that—the solution. Rather than focusing on the problem, complaining and whining, focus on the answer to the problem. Yes, you need to be able to identify the problem first. But once you do, shift your focus from the problem or the obstacle and onto the solution. Don't think, "Oh, my gosh, it's raining," and stop there. Get your umbrella out: problem solved. You're not going to get wet now.

Make changes based on the solution. Don't make changes based on the problem. Rather than saying, "Oh, my gosh, I'm so tired," do something to solve it. Go to bed early. "Oh, my kids are bothering me." What do they want? Some connection with you? A snack? Make that happen. Look to the how can I. How can I solve this problem? How can I start liking something I don't like? How can I change that thing around so that I don't engage in negative self-talk? Ask yourself, what's the solution? How can I make it better?

4. Feeling Small around Others
The number four killer of your confidence is feeling small around others—a little case of the old compare-itis. I'm sure you've been there and can relate. I'm going to give you some great solutions.

Solutions to Feeling Small
One way you can feel more confident is by dressing the part. Dress to impress. If you have your hair done and accessories on and nice clothes, you'll feel more the part. I'm not saying you need to go and buy the most expensive clothes. All I'm suggesting is you need to feel confident in the clothes that you are wearing. You should be dressing for the level of success and confidence that you want. You'd never show up at a grand event wearing your jeans. So always make sure you show up

wearing something that makes you feel good because that will come across to others.

The second is stand tall, focus on your posture. Posture says so much non-verbally about your confidence. Often you will see people who roll their shoulders forward, making them appear as though they're smaller or even trying to make themselves disappear. Even if the person is smiling or outgoing, you can sense something is off. It changes your perception of them. A little trick is to throw your shoulders up as high as they will go, roll them back and drop them.

Try doing it now if you haven't already. Do it again. Shoulders up, rollback, drop and stick out your chest. That immediately changes your posture. In comparison, when your posture is poor, you exhibit lower self-esteem, lower self-confidence, and you are not in a powerful stance. Also, having your arms at your sides or moving and open when you talk is better than crossed arms.

I have noticed many people place their hands behind their backs when they stand to ask questions, at a microphone or are introducing themselves. Standing with your hands behind your back is a victim stance, a stance of service and servitude. Instead, shoulders back, stand tall with your arms at your side, and your chin straight. Please don't put your chin up in the air, because remember; we are not trying to portray a massive ego or arrogance. When you are talking to someone, maintain eye contact. Looking at a person in the eye shows confidence. This may not be the case for certain cultures, as I found when I lived in Japan for three years and worked for a Korean Company for six. I learned pretty quickly people don't look straight in your eyes unless they are an equal or higher up than you in a hierarchy.

But in the Western World, looking people in the eyes is a sign of respect, respect for them and respect for yourself.

Choose to look at people in the eyes rather than looking down at your shoes or looking beyond their faces. That's not showing confidence. Yes, it's sometimes uncomfortable to stare at somebody the whole time we're talking, and you don't want to maintain such strict eye contact that it feels strange. We naturally look away briefly and think for a second, but make sure your eyes meet theirs, again and again, each time you look away. Eye contact creates connection, and that connection displays confidence because you are willing and able and confident enough to be seen.

Another thing you can do to show you are confident is to speak slowly. When you talk slowly, people listen to what you say because you make it seem more important. You are using pauses to highlight the essential pieces. If I was standing on stage, I could use a slower pace as a way of pulling in the audience and getting them to lean in and listen a little bit closer. However, when I'm on video, my goal is to be highly engaging and ooze high energy because I've already built a rapport with my viewers.

On video, I'm trying to pack a lot of information into one sitting. To share it as quickly as possible because your ears and brain are processing it all a lot faster than if I was to speak slowly.

Another reason I do this is to make sure you are not multitasking. By speaking faster, I know that I have your attention a little bit more than speaking slowly.

5. Feel like a Fraud
Killer confidence number five is that you feel unqualified, or you feel like a fraud. I get that a lot of times when people talk about starting their own business. I want to discuss three ways you can boost your confidence in regards to feeling like a fraud. Often, we think we are under-qualified or that we are frauds, but we have to own where we are in our situation. If you start

a business and go to an event where people are further ahead of you, acknowledge that you are new, don't try to fake experience. You will gain experience as you go along.

3 Solutions so You Don't Feel like a Fraud

1. Be Prepared. If you're telling yourself, "Oh, I'm new to this whole business thing," make sure you at least know how to explain what you do and what you are looking for. Spend some time with that. If you are in a panel or an interview where you will be answering questions, be prepared for how you will respond. It might take a little bit more learning. Remember the first time you drove a car? It felt like, "Okay, I need to put on my seatbelt, I need to check the rear-view mirror, I need to check the side mirror and over my shoulder before switching lanes." Every part of it felt awkward, and you had to remind yourself of what to do step by step. But the more time you spent driving and as the years passed, all these things eventually became so natural they are now second nature. The more you prepare yourself, the readier you will be. The more you prepare and the more you hone your skills, the more automatic it becomes.

2. Increase Your Competency. When you become more competent, you're going to feel like you fit in more. You are going to feel like you earned it. Do you feel unqualified? What is it you feel unable to do? Whether it's your competency on the yoga mat or in your sales calls. You have options. You can read more about it. Seek opportunities to study it in a course or program. Practice with and learn from others. Just figure out what you're not skilled at or still need to master. Write it down. Then ask yourself questions about how you can get there, focusing on becoming more competent in using the skills to become more confident.

3. Empower Yourself with Knowledge. The last part of this is to become more knowledgeable. What topic or area do you need to gain more knowledge? The rules of golf? Aspects of your industry? You can read books, listen to podcasts, and do research. Maybe you prefer to hire somebody to teach you. Whatever you need to do, do it. Learn more so that when you speak, you feel confident that what you are saying is true.

After you learn the knowledge, it's about practicing presenting it or discussing it or sharing it, hone what you need to do with the information. You are unshakable when you have experience, preparation, and knowledge.

6. Scared of Failure and Success

Sometimes people are just scared of doing something new. Is that you? Are you afraid of the next big step, or are you scared because you don't know the next step? I hear this so many times.

When you are afraid of success, you're not fearful of achieving great results; you're scared of what great results will do to you, who you are as a person, your values, relationships, priorities, and life.

People don't walk around saying, "I'm afraid of having lots of money, I'm scared of having ideal clients. I'm fearful of finding the right partner." It's more like, "I'm afraid the money is going to change me, I'm scared that because of all of the success, all the people around me won't love me anymore."

I have been asked, "How can we know if we have a fear of success?" When I asked the ladies who were going through the program to put their hands up if they fear success, more than half went up.

Solutions to Fear of Failure and Success

Instead of focusing on being scared of failure and scared of success, focus on the result of what could happen. Just focus on the next step, on completing the task. Focus on getting yourself closer to reaching your goal. As you go along the path, your confidence in completing each step will get you ready for this part.

I was the keynote speaker at a massive conference in Washington. I was being flown in, and a great many women were paying to be there and see me. That can seem pretty scary, but I thought I'm just at the starting point when I was hired. I haven't done all the preparation, all the planning, all the knowledge-seeking, all the competency training to prepare yet, so I'm not thinking about standing on stage. I'm thinking about what I will be delivering and how I'll deliver it. And after all of that, then I'm going to practice my delivery. As you do each step, and as you are successful at each little step, you'll feel confident doing that step again.

If we talk about business, the first time you pick up the phone to cold call somebody is scary. But the second time will be a little less risky. Over time, you kind of look back and you go, "Oh, my, why was I ever nervous about that? That was so easy. I'm a pro now."

When I was beginning, offering my products and coaching was scary, and networking was scary. But now I often hear from clients is, "Oh, that's so insightful. You just said that so easily. Can you repeat it so I can write it down?"

Don't be afraid of the result. Instead of fearing what could happen if you don't do everything just right, have greater fear in doing nothing at all. Just sitting there and doing nothing sucks, it's terrible, and it's going to kill your confidence.

Don't let failure be the focus of your fears. Failure is part of the learning process. Everyone fails at some point, especially the most successful people in the world. Take the word "failure" out of your vocabulary because if you give that to your inner saboteur, they are just going to run with it. Never give up. Again, failure is not an option. Don't accept defeat. Just think, there's a solution to this. What's the solution? What's the answer to get past this obstacle? If your first idea for a solution doesn't work, ask yourself, well, what's my solution to that? As you succeed, you'll learn that adversity will always co-exist with challenges. When you learn to anticipate obstacles and anticipate your success in the face of obstacles, you will experience an even more significant boost of confidence.

7. Being Indecisive

The last killer of confidence is indecisiveness. Going with somebody else's opinion or sticking with the majority even though you oppose it. When you don't trust yourself and place yourself in a position where you give in and go with what someone else wants, you enter that Power Under position. Anyone in Power Over is going to be able to take advantage of you.

You can also risk sitting in limbo, telling yourself, "Maybe I should do this, or maybe I should do that." I've seen limbo occur with clients when they state, "I'm going to do this, and I'm going to do that and this and this and this and this because I can't just decide on one." If you are trying to do everything or can't decide because you're too worried you'll make the wrong choice, you will not get very far.

Solutions to Be Decisive

I encourage you to get past this by being assertive. Stand up for what you believe. Stick to your principles. By choosing a path and staying on it, you will keep the course. If the path changes, that's okay, but you must stand in that new way with confidence. Flexibility is essential because people change their minds all the time. Life is full of change. I change my mind when I see that something is not optimal, whether in my personal life or a business decision. Maybe I changed, or perhaps it was my circumstances that changed. If you alter the way, stand in that. Don't let anyone change you back to how it was before. If you genuinely believe in this new way forward, stay the course. Know your values and live with them.

I run a program called Dynamic Balance™, where we go through your values and priorities to create dynamic goals in every area of your life. The clients I work with one-on-one know values are essential. I don't mean morals; I mean your values. Your confidence comes when you stand steadfast and stay true to what you believe. One time I was in line to make a purchase in a store, and I noticed the person ahead of me shoplifting. I couldn't just standby and keep it to myself because I knew that this was a charity shop. The money raised was for charity. Even if it wasn't for charity, I couldn't ignore what I was seeing. I was shocked at what was happening. I was even more appalled that though others could see the shoplifting, no one said anything to the cashier who was too busy to notice. The shoplifter put some items on the counter, but she could slip other items that she hadn't paid for into her bag because the counter was so high.

I was standing there thinking, "What do I do?" I knew that if I didn't say anything, this would just haunt me for the rest of the day or the week or for a long time. I made eye contact with the person and standing in my confidence, I said, "I see what you are doing." I didn't say, "You are shoplifting. Stop it." I said, "I see what you are doing." I allowed her to fix it. She didn't admit to it, and so I said, "Okay, I see what you are doing. I see you are putting things in your bag as you put things on the counter." No one spoke up. No one said anything. No one backed me up. At that point, I could have just backed down and apologized for bothering her.

When in your life, have you wished you could stand up a little bit stronger? When in your life, have you stood up strong to somebody else because something wasn't right? Just think of how important that was to you. With my story in the charity shop, at that moment, it was important to me that I stood up and I said something. She did admit she 'accidentally' put a few things in her bag, and so she pulled them back out and put them on the counter to pay for them. When she left, I told the cashier, "I had to say something." He silently mouthed to me, "Thank you."

But the people behind me said, "You don't know their situation." I got a lot of flak for speaking up, but I knew I needed to say something. Stand up for what you believe. Stand up for what is right and wrong. Don't just stand up for other people; stand up for yourself. If something is not right, stand up for yourself. It doesn't mean that you have to be angry or yell. Get into your confidence pose and make eye contact. Speak slowly if you need to and come from that place of, "These are my values, and these are my guidelines, my priorities, and I'm standing strong in them."

I did have to go and chat with her because my curiosity and empathy kicked in. Was she struggling? Could she not afford the items? Did she need help? In the parking lot, I approached her to get to know her story. I was ready to give her some money if she needed it, but she said she was okay. I asked again. She said she was fine, then lighting up a cigarette, she denied she had stolen anything, which confirmed I had done the right thing.

This story could be seen only as a moral issue, that of stealing. But I also speak up when people use racist remarks when people cut in front of me in line when there is a faster way to do something. All my actions stem from my values of respect for others, equality and efficiency.

When you are clear on your values, you can make better decisions faster, with more clarity and confidence.

Birds of a Feather Flock Together

Generally speaking, people are attracted to others who are confident. If you want to be confident, hang around confident people. Let it rub off on you, and you will attract people who want to be around you because of your confidence. I just want to share one more thing. Have you ever seen a speaker on stage who you knew was super nervous and felt for her? Maybe you stopped listening to her message because your heart was going out to her and wanting her to succeed and wanting her not to be so nervous.

Think about how you feel when you are around somebody who you know isn't confident. It's the same feeling. You struggle to listen to the message because you're too busy worrying about how and what they feel. We all want to be standing in our full confidence.

Here's Your Quick Win for Confidence

Knowing where you are confident is a great place to start to have a quick win for confidence. Write up a list of 25 things where you show up confidently. You can focus on actions, skills, experiences, ways of being, and something you have accomplished.

I want to check-in. How are you feeling right now about coming up with that list? Did your brain go, "Oh, my gosh, that's too many! I don't know if I can complete that!"? Negative self-talk. Are you coming down with compare-itis? Did you sink into yourself and lose your good posture? What is it? Were you judging yourself? Did it just feel overwhelming? Did any of these seven killers come into play as you read this challenge?

Do it on your own first. Come back to it a couple of times and then if you still need more, you ask others, "Can you tell me what I'm good at? Can you tell me why I'm great? Can you tell me what I've achieved?"

Here are some examples from some of my clients:
- "I'm confident brainstorming."
- "I'm confident at organizing events."
- "I'm confident learning new things."
- "I am confident relating to many different people."

If you're stuck and are having a hard time making a list of 25 reasons why you are fantastic, start with any of your massive achievements, then go on to smaller accomplishments that came along the way. Ask yourself what helped me get there? Then you'll see some of the other places you can now be confident! Here are some ideas from the massive achievement of, "I'm confident closing deals and I closed 20 big deals this year."
- I'm confident writing sales script.
- I'm confident making cold calls.
- I'm confident with new sales techniques.
- I'm a master at follow-up.

This list is now a great way to boost motivation, future confidence and creative ways of getting better results in the future.

That's the end of the seven killers of confidence. Now is the time for you to stand in the seven solutions, the seven ways to boost your confidence over the next week. Let me know what works. Let me know your experiences, which ones are easy for you, which ones are a little bit harder, and don't forget to ask for support.

To learn more about the other 8 Pillars within the Dynamic You™ program or participate in group coaching to experience more in-depth and more profound shifts in your confidence go to www.dianerolston.com.

I congratulate you on completing this section. I know you will get so much out of the rest of the book. When you read take notes, implement the learning and check out each author's links and profiles.

Stay Dynamic!
~ Diane

"YOU'RE
DYNAMIC!
BE
UNAPOLOGETICALLY
YOU!"

~ DIANE ROLSTON

NOW BEGINS
THE CONTRIBUTIONS
FROM TOP THOUGHT LEADERS,
EXPERTS & DYNAMIC WOMEN®!

The accomplished entrepreneurs and professionals were selected for the book because of their commitment to serving others and willingness to share their secrets for living a Confident life.

You get to choose how to read them: All in one sitting. One Confidence Secret a day or One Confidence Secret a week. With 33 contributors and the Confidence Training by Diane Rolston, doing one a week works, but in the end it's all up to you.

Just get started!

CONFIDENCE SECRET #1
From Hobby to a Profitable Business
Anahita Shahrvini

In 2010 I teamed up with my mother and created GogoBags, a line of reusable bags that keep food fresh for longer. They are simple yet effective everyday bags with beautiful fun prints and smart fabrics. Within a few years, we took this ordinary product, despite the odds, from our first show at a small local Christmas craft market to a well-known and established brand, selling in stores like Wholefoods, Nesters, and Amazon. And we did that with confidence!

It was not easy. We made mistakes and learnt from them; that is why I am confident that I can show you how to turn your hobby and talent into a profitable business in simple, practical steps.

Here are three secrets to start your profitable craft business with confidence:

#1-Decide on your story
As crafters, we focus more on our craft rather than our story. We all have a story; what is yours? Find that edge that makes you shine.

#2-Focus on benefits rather than features
Customers care more about the benefits of your products than their features. What is in it for them?

#3-Know your numbers
Track everything, especially at the beginning when you hit the craft markets. It's important to know what you paid for the table, the hours you spent working in the market, how much

you sold and the hours you worked to get ready for the show. This information is a must to measure if you are profitable.

Crafters usually underestimate the time and effort they put in doing their craft and miss adding that to their pricing. Having the right price point and considering all the costs that go into a product is essential. I discuss these aspects of pricing in detail in my e-book 7 Steps to a Profitable Craft Business, available free on my website.

_____

Anahita Shahrvini was born into an entrepreneurial family, she has been running either her family's or her own business since she was 19. With her passion for creation, she turned her hobby into a 6-figure business, and that led her to help others do the same in her coaching business and is "Helping Makers Make Money".

Email: anahita@anahitashahrvini.com
Instagram: @anahitashahrvini
Website: www.anahitashahrvini.com

CONFIDENCE SECRET #2
It's No Secret at All
Candace Hollas

My secret is really no secret at all. We all know how to be confident because we teach our children to be confident. It hit me most when my daughter was suddenly afraid of something that she'd been doing for years, and we worked for over a year for her confidence to "return."

My 11-year-old daughter is amazing. She is strong (both physically and emotionally), smart, creative, super brave, funny and is one of the most kind-hearted, thoughtful, and grateful humans. Confident as can be.

I tell my daughter that she's brave, that I'm proud of her, and I believe in her. I remind her that she is strong and can make good decisions. I teach her not to accept negativity or unwarranted criticism from others or herself. When I see it happen, we talk about how the negativity and negative self-talk is affecting her life. And when I see positivity, I celebrate with her and help her bask in how good it feels to be positive. She knows how outcomes can be altered by a change in attitude and being confident in yourself.

When she faces challenges and confidence wanes, I remind my daughter of her hard work: the ups and the downs. The hundreds of times, she practiced achieving a new skill. I remind her of her past successes, and even the disappointments she has overcome. I asked her what she would say to a younger person in her shoes and ask her why she does not give herself that same grace. Her ability to advise herself gains confidence.

When she compares herself to others, I remind her that it's all about her. It's her efforts, her mind, her body, her soul, her confidence.

I support her and teach her to be confident and strong. And she IS.

Then, I remind myself and give myself the same grace I give my daughter. I remind myself that I, too, am confident. I'm teaching it every single day.

Candace Hollas is the owner of Our Zesty Life, and Business Manager of SWP Media Ltd. SWP Media Ltd. operates multiple recipe websites, and Candace works on the business side, behind the scenes. As a Chartered Professional Accountant (CPA, CGA) with an extensive marketing background, she is the perfect fit for a dynamic, growing company.

Candace's strong experience in business, accounting, finance, process, people management, and marketing all play a role in her work with the owner and team at SWP Media. All this while running a side hustle!

Candace is a mother of two, a wife, sister, and dedicated friend. Her passions lie in numbers, cooking, travel, family, and fun!

Email: candacehollas@gmail.com
Facebook: @candace.hollas
Website: www.ourzestylife.com

CONFIDENCE SECRET #3
Embrace Your Shadows
Cassedi Carlsen

For me, courage is speaking my truth in each moment with love, regardless of how others might respond. This year I learnt to be with my shadows and accept them without attempting to change them or push them down.

At the age of five, my best friend Samantha and I were inseparable. We played soccer together, had sleepovers, inside jokes and nicknames. As we started to get older, Samantha deepened her connection with some of the 'popular' kids in school. Eventually, in order to appease her friends, she renounced our friendship and publicly embarrassed me.

As a result of feeling abandoned and betrayed, I adopted the ever-present attitude of a person socially shunned; I got mean. Rather than carrying on being myself, I over-analyzed every social situation. I found out how to best protect myself from ridicule and control my environment, which led to anxiety and lots of negativity.

Recently, I got an opportunity to face and release this deep subconscious wound. Delving into the subconscious suffering from my childhood was painful. Fortunately, I felt well equipped and supported. I realized I had been preparing for this my entire life. Every event had put me here. I was able to be with my seven-year-old self, feel how she felt, and help her choose a new way to respond with unconditional love for self and others.

That child and this courageous adult know how wonderful they are because they are themselves. And they deepen that self-love every day. Life has gotten unfathomably richer as a result of learning to speak the truth in each moment.

By accepting myself, and all that I am, I permit everyone to seek and embody more of who they already are. Learning to acknowledge and witness the turbulence in life helps me extract all of the lessons and integrate them with grace. When we charge into the darkest parts of ourselves with courage and accept it all, unconditional love prevails, and we prosper.

Cassedi Carlsen is an intuitive bodywork and energetic alignment practitioner, event facilitator, and conscious kids program creator. Her focus is on educating students on energy management and intuitive living.

Cassedi provides clients with a wide array of tools and personalized strategies to help them take responsibility for their health and wellness. Tools such as intuitive eating, breathwork, meditation, energy healing, aromatherapy, massage, myofascial release yoga/ movement, sound healing and more!

Email: cassedicarlsen@gmail.com
Facebook: @aaromaflowhealing
Instagram: @aaroma_flow_healing

CONFIDENCE SECRET #4
Tough Conversations Causing Fear and Anxiety? The Key to a Positive Outcome for Everyone
Corina Stainsby

As a former Occupational Therapist who has worked with injured clients facing the realities of their disabilities, I've taken part in many difficult conversations. Things haven't changed much now that I'm a Realtor and a Seniors Consultant, helping older adults address ageing challenges. Seniors coping with growing health and safety concerns, along with feelings of losing control over their independence, can make discussions about making changes in their lives more difficult.

Thankfully, experience has been a kind teacher. I've learned that you can confidently tackle sensitive topics with anyone if you practice active empathy when interacting with others.

Conversations become uncomfortable when we feel that the other person won't agree with what we have to say. It's essential to show that we are here as much to listen as we are to speak.

By reminding ourselves that we're trying to help (as opposed to trying to 'win'), we become open to seeing another point of view. Other strategies include using "I feel..." rather than a confrontational "You did..." statement. Also, asking open-ended questions invites the other person to lower their defences and speak their mind. To keep the discussion positive and collaborative, we can ask questions like, "What would it mean to you if you had to stop driving?" The goal here is to problem-solve together through dialogue, not dictate the solution or to convince through arguments.

This approach also lets us express opposing views more sensitively. We can frame our opinions to acknowledge and tell the other person their feelings are valuable. Saying, "I understand why this is important to you, but I feel this is also important...," offers a bridge between the divide.

Ultimately, when faced with a difficult conversation ahead, you can't go wrong when you lead from the heart.

Corina Stainsby is a Seniors Real Estate Specialist and founder of Heart and Home, a company dedicated to helping older Canadians love where they live.

She ventured into Real Estate, wanting to bring her personal brand of empathy to the industry. Heart and Home provides housing options and strategies so that Seniors can live life on their terms. Whether it be moving to a home that meets their needs or adapting their home to age in place, her guide, "Should I Move or Stay?" helps Seniors navigate these difficult questions. Connect with Corina by email for your free copy.

Email: corina@heartnhome.ca
Facebook: @corina.stainsby
Website: www.heartnhome.ca

CONFIDENCE SECRET #5
Retrain Your Brain; How to find Inner Peace and Release Your Existing Confidence
Eleni Christina

Do you remember the last time you were genuinely carefree? Carefree and confident? For me, I was about 12 years old, confident in my abilities to follow my dreams. I'm slowly starting to find that girl again. I've been bringing her back into my life via Guided Meditation.

I'm learning to let go of the past, releasing the grip that the dark moments in life have exerted. Through guided meditation, I am anchoring myself in peace. I have comfort in knowing that I am right where I am supposed to be. Meditation eases my anxiety and heightens my confidence far more than I could ever have imagined.

When I first started guided meditation, don't get me wrong, I was still making those to-do lists in my mind. My thoughts always intruded; however, with practice, aromatherapy and honouring the use of crystals and stones, I have retrained my brain to turn off intrusive thoughts.

Want to know a secret? You can release your existing confidence also. It doesn't have to be through meditation; it just has to be with something that truly brings you happiness and peace. A daily practice that allows you to turn off all of those negative thoughts, worries and stressors. Love to dance? Take 5 min a day to dedicate to your favourite tunes; shut the world out. Even if it's just for five minutes, you and your 12-year-old self deserve it.

Eleni Christina is an entrepreneur and local artisan from Mission, BC. Shop Lily Dawn is Eleni's successful jewelry and apparel business; her creativity shines through in her unique designs. The collection includes an assortment of jewelry, which harnesses stones and crystals' power and healing energy. Eleni also designs extremely comfy, cozy and fun apparel.

Shop Lily Dawn has flourished after her daughter's birth in 2018 when Eleni chose to turn her hobby into a full-time gig. She is a passionate supporter of Canadian businesses and ensures that all materials used throughout her entire creative process are sourced within Canada. All stones used in Eleni's work are Grade A Gemstones and, when used properly, can provide an abundance of healing for the wearer. Eleni recommends handling all stones with care and setting your intentions for each piece of jewelry you choose to wear for the day.

Email: info@shoplilydawn.ca
Instagram: @shoplilydawn
Website: www.shoplilydawn.ca

CONFIDENCE SECRET #6
Fake it Until You Make It
Erin Johnstone

Growing up, I knew I was different. I was sensitive and highly intuitive. I was also very insecure. I had some very challenging moments; I was teased as a child, told I looked like a boy, and in my teens; bullied. As a young adult, I had a desperate desire to be accepted, fit in, and be like everyone else. At 13 years old and in high school, I started to develop extreme anxiety; after grade ten, it was a real struggle. Speaking up in groups, being on the spot, even walking into a room was a dreaded and challenging task.

Fast forward 20 years, I started having panic attacks, a constant flood of negative thoughts. Worries, fears, self-deprecating thoughts and worst-case scenarios filled my mind. It was in my journey to heal myself and change my anxious mind that I discovered hypnotherapy. After a few sessions, I was amazed and in disbelief of the shifts in my thought processes, compared to the years of prior work. I knew I had found my purpose. Two months later, I was enrolled in school to become a certified hypnotherapist.

Hypnotherapy isn't precisely your mainstream type of therapy. When I graduated school, I distinctly remember someone saying to me, "You can't possibly make any money at that." At that moment, something inside me altered. Perhaps it was my knowledge of the mind. Maybe it was all the hypnotherapy in school that shifted my beliefs; I began to adopt a "feel the fear do it anyway" attitude. I would affirm to myself, "Fake it until you make it," and "I can handle anything!" I began to accept myself for all of me, the good, the bad and the ugly, even if others didn't.

All of that positive self-talk created confidence in myself, a deeper trust in my connection to the universe and a belief that I absolutely CAN handle anything. The proof is that I have built a successful business and I am fulfilling both my financial and professional goals. I couldn't believe the first time my client booking was full, five weeks in advance!

Life holds many growth opportunities, and each challenge brings up old limiting beliefs, and in those moments, we have the chance to change. Visualize yourself how you want to be, breathe in the feeling of confidence, and you will become THAT!

Erin Johnstone is a professional clinical hypnotherapist. Educated in 2014, she earned her Clinical Hypnotherapy Certification. She has additional certifications in "HypnoDontics," and she is a HypnoBirthing® - The Mongan Method Child Birth Educator.

Email: info@healingsoulhypnosis.com
Facebook: @healingsoulhypnosis
Website: www.healingsoulhypnosis.com

CONFIDENCE SECRET #7
Confidence Leads to Success.
I am Confident; Therefore, I am Successful!
Erin Kellie

Social media is a powerful and effective tool to bring in new business and clients. The most amazing part of it is that you are in control of the narrative. You decide what and how people see you online & it's free.

Self-confidence is an amazing thing and has a huge impact on ones' success. Let's face it. At the very least, you will need to believe in your own skills, goals, and ability to succeed, or you won't be able to show up, right? Beyond this, people want to buy from those who are confident and believable. Therefore, we could say, confidence leads to success.

So, what leads to confidence? I would say it lies in knowing and accepting yourself. It all begins with understanding what your core values are. As such, I suggest taking the time to really figure them out. You must know your values well enough that you are aware of where to draw the line as not to cross or contradict it.

Believe it or not, the key to success in business is aligning what you are selling with your authentic core values, and then the confidence flows naturally!

Be firm with your values, stand for and against things; it's ok to have an opinion but be consistent and deliver with integrity. It is not about winning or being right but rather just having the conversation and determining if you share values with your audience.

These interactions are great opportunities for your audience to get to know you better. They will be able to identify your core values, making an informed decision to work together. Honestly, being your authentic self, employing respect and kindness will not only grow your confidence it will also increase your integrity with your audience.

The goal of social media is to surround yourself with your people. You know the ones you want to work with and who also want to work with you.

Do not mourn the loss of followers. You want to spend your time with the people whose values align with yours, and losing followers is one way to know you are doing it right.

Show up consistently online, posting content and answering questions. Engage, engage, oh and engage. Just believe in yourself and share it with others online, and your ideal soulmate clients will find you!

Erin Kellie is the founder of Coastal Blue Media, a social media marketing and brand experience boutique located on the Sunshine Coast of BC, Canada. When she isn't glued to a computer, she is a busy mom to her three children. Her career has been primarily focused on her passion, aiding small businesses with marketing and brand development.

Facebook: @ErinPKellie
Facebook: @CoastalBlueMedia
Website: www.CoastalBlueMedia.com

CONFIDENCE SECRET #8
Improve Your Confidence
and Increase Your Net Worth
Estrellita Gonzalez

If someone told my younger self that I would one day be a politician, entrepreneur and crypto-currency educator, I wouldn't have believed them. I was a shy girl with little confidence. Since then, I have learned to step into the feeling, gain self-awareness and the confidence to do anything I desire.

At fifteen, my father bought a restaurant, and I became a server. I was nervous and terrified! I recall one customer, not very impressed with me and my serving skills, called me boring. Isn't it funny we can vividly remember when people put us down? While I was upset, I recognized I didn't want this; it became a subliminal motivator.

Girls generally gain confidence through their fathers, but I didn't. As I later embarked on a corporate career in a man's world, I started to work on myself through books, retreats and seminars; self-awareness and greater confidence took hold.

Ten years ago, as a single parent wanting more control of my schedule, I started my skincare clinic. Early on, I questioned whether I was on the right track; the self-doubt held me back. To tackle this, I worked with coaches. As I tweaked my business, worked on my mindset and got my vision clear, things fell into place. I became aligned with my values, purpose and the message I had to share.

I have studied money and wealth for years. Recently I jumped into the new, male-dominated world of crypto-currency. While this brought me back to my unsure 15-year-old self, I stepped into the fear faithfully. My passion for creating passive income buoyed me. I now offer crypto-currency programs for women to feel confident and empowered about their money.

Here are three things you can do to build your confidence:
1. Get clear on your vision, values and purpose.
2. Focus on what you want and take action.
3. Have a daily positive mindset.

As I raised my son and grew my business, these actions also guided me to run for political office, winning not once but twice. Everything I do today I have created; I know I can create what I desire. My message to you: believe in yourself, and your natural confidence will shine through.

Estrellita Gonzalez's values on health and wellbeing guide her days and work. She is a politician, owns the successful Derma Bright Clinic and runs multiple wellness companies. As a digital wealth investor and educator, she supports women in building their net worth through passive income.

Facebook: @EstieMartin
LinkedIn: @estrellitagonzalez
Website: www.estrellitagonzalez.com

CONFIDENCE SECRET #9
Box Up Your Inner Freakazoid
Heather Spooner

I have an inner freakazoid. (I'll pretend I'm normal and presume everyone does). When jumping out of my comfort zone, I see myself in my mind's eye, with multiple limbs flailing in anatomically impossible directions. A monosyllabic scream carried along with the dust cloud encircling this cartoon version of myself. Externally, I'm cool as a cucumber, of course. (Unless you're my family- God bless them- to whom my frantic emotions are as evident to as my mismatched pajamas).

So, with transitioning from nursing to owning a business online, my freakazoid had a heyday because the comparison of those careers is like an apple to...a horse. Confidence in my business model? I never wavered. Confidence in my unique ability to succeed? It wavered like a lit flame in the wind.

Eventually, I gained some skills for boxing up that freakazoid party before she took up permanent residence and invited unwanted house guests.

First: don't think, do. If you're reasonably sure your decision will improve, not harm, your business, act on it. Fast. In the online world, this equates to one quick click of the mouse. It's relatively easy to move one little finger if you don't overthink it. Most times, once in cyberspace, you can't take it back. Problem solved.

Second: jump out of ONE comfort zone at a time. Leaving a comfort zone to accomplish a necessary step to success creates vulnerability and stress. But forward progress breeds confidence, and confidence, in turn, breeds success. So, we must leave comfort zones in a manageable way. For me, that's one at a time.

Does my freakazoid still throw fits? Yeah, sure. I'm human, even if she's not. (Hahaha!) But currently, she's confined to a box: Party decorations and all.

Heather Spooner realized life was passing by with minimal goals met despite having a full-time nursing career. She also craved a life without night shifts and fixed schedules. The dreary thought of continuing on the same path until retirement pushed her to rethink her plans.

After watching her best friend, who was consistently achieving inspiring success online, she decided to watch the information webinar and research the opportunity. Informed and with prayer, she became an online business owner without regrets.

Today Heather coaches others through a proven, successful training program used by thousands worldwide for running a business online. She is thrilled to have taken charge of reinventing her future and is helping others do the same.

Email: info@heatherspooner.ca
Facebook: @heatherlianalive
Website: www.heatherspooner.ca

CONFIDENCE SECRET #10
Take the Step
Ilona Pretorius

"Measure Twice, Cut Once" is something my Dad used to say to us when he worked on making items that we would use in and around the house. His words remind us that we should not blindly rush into things but evaluate and then take action on the evaluation. I learnt there is a cost for doing something without planning, but there is also a cost for not doing anything.

When we decided we wanted to move to Canada, we reviewed the requirements, got our applications ready and submitted them. The wait for the Canadian Government response felt very long, but once we got the answer, we wrapped up things and made arrangements to ship our belongings and moved.

Starting fresh in Canada was a fun experience and allowed us opportunities we could not have anticipated. The biggest one was when my husband suggested we purchase a small business from the lady who started it and wanted to retire. We did the evaluation and took the step to buy. Talk about learning a lot of new things very fast. Even now every day allows us and our team and to learn and grow.

In life and business there will be areas where we must start at the very beginning and areas where we ask for support. The benefit is it allows us to stay humble. You can do a lot, but not everything. Choose to take the step and don't forget to "Measure Twice, Cut Once"

Ilona Pretorius is a wife and Mother of two adult boys and two dogs have been living In Langley, B.C. for more than ten years. Ilona and her husband moved to Canada in the mid-1990s, starting in Vancouver, and moving East as their multi-generational family needed more space in their house.

Ilona Is an Entrepreneur by heart. In her day job, she supports the implementation of ERP's (Enterprise Resource Planning) for Asset Intensive, Project Manufacturing or Repetitive Manufacturing organizations.

The family side hustle is the micro food manufacturing company, Edible Coast, which operates with a small staff in Surrey, B.C. Edible Coast produces Gone Crackers and Gone Kooky products.

Email: Ilona-pretorius@outlook.com
LinkedIn: @ilonapretorius
Website: www.ediblecoast.com

CONFIDENCE SECRET #11
Will the Real YOU, Please Stand Up!
Jacquie Rougeau

Sadly, we worry so much about pleasing others or what other people think about us. Have you felt this? We create judgments in our own heads. We read emotions into situations where it doesn't exist. We over-analyze Facebook messages or comments made by others.

I do this. Do you? You see, people tell me I'm too much for them, and others say I am not enough. I'm equal parts loud and quiet. I'm career-driven and wildly fun. I have been a corporate employee, and now I am an entrepreneur. I'm all of these things. I am truly me. I used to try so hard to bend myself many different ways to fit into an ever-changing preformed shape, hoping to fit in somehow. But why? For what? Approval? To be liked?

You can never be enough when you constantly shape-shift for others. It is endless and empty. I say no more! I give you permission to be YOU. Authentically you! You are living YOUR life! Your journey!!!

If you laugh too loudly or people don't get your sense of humour, who cares. If you are quiet and people think you are stuck up, that's their loss. If you want to work, work. If your purpose is to be a stay-at-home parent or grandparent, then do it. If creating or writing, hiking tall mountains or anything else brings you joy, then do it! If you didn't make that meal or cake from scratch but instead ran to the grocery store to pick it up, don't fret it.

You can choose how you live your life. You're not in a box. Be you. Do you. Just be the best at whatever you want to be!

Don't be afraid to go against the tide; to do your own thing without quitting.

Focus on your passion, the one that sets your soul on fire, regardless of what others think. Be who you are, not who others want you to be because you're never going to be everything for everyone, just like I'm not. You have my permission to be YOU! But actually, you never needed it in the first place.

Jacquie Rougeau is passionate about good food, healthy living, and positively impacting others' lives. She is a vibrant leader nurturing and challenging her team to develop, achieve and exceed their goals. She is a fun-loving mom with three adult children and is also a "Mamere" to four entertaining grandchildren.

After dealing with the devastating ending of her 33-year marriage, she focused on her growth to eventually become unapologetically herself. Jacquie rose and grew through the pain. She harnessed her growth to kick life up into full gear. She has transformed her "hobby" business to become a Senior Director in Epicure, leading a large team of consultants both in Canada and the United States. She loves going live and teaching cooking classes in her VIP Customer Group: www.facebook.com/groups/jacquierougeauvips

Jacquie is in her second chapter after transitioning from a successful career in the banking industry. As an enthusiastic traveler, Jacquie has proven that her business success doesn't mean sticking close to home. She is jumping into the RV lifestyle, eager to explore North America. You can see her RV at www.facebook.com/jacquie.rougeau.spice.diva.

Jacquie won't be alone on her adventures: her love joins her; he is her partner in crime through all things fun and challenging and is her biggest supporter. She is profoundly grateful for the life she has created. Jacquie's love of life comes through, no matter what she is doing, from hanging with her children and grandchildren, experiencing travel adventures, or working her Epicure business. Jacquie plans to continue her cooking classes from her RV, be assured that fun, laughter and love will continue to be her signature style.

Email: spicedivaceo@gmail.com
Instagram: @spicedivaceo
Website: https://jacquierougeau.epicure.com/en-ca

"THE EASIEST WAY TO **BUILD** **CONFIDENCE** IS TO **TAKE ACTION** TOWARDS A GOAL – EVEN A SMALL ONE."

~ *Diane Rolston*

CONFIDENCE SECRET #12
The Perfect Recipe for Confidence
Jess Callegaro

Have you ever watched someone walk into a room radiating with confidence? They didn't even speak, and yet, they glowed? Perhaps you said to yourself, "I want whatever they ate for breakfast!" Are you nodding your head up and down right now?

Girlfriend, listen to me -what she ate for breakfast wasn't a bowl of gluten-free magic corn puffs. It was self-development, grit and an unwavering belief in her purpose. And that recipe is available for anyone to devour who's willing to put in the work, including you.

I'm going to share a personal story with you about pivoting with purpose and passion. I was that girl who thought she needed a prestigious degree and a fancy job to be confident. Yet, when I eventually landed it all, I felt wholly paralyzed from stamping a time clock and trapped by legislative rules.

Here is my pivot - I up and quit the career I had worked six years to establish. I left to become an online health coach. And to set the record straight, I was not confident about this new profession. I had no certification, I had no website, and I had no idea who my clients would be. But, I had this unwavering belief in myself. I knew that if I poured everything I had into this new business and mixed in my passion, the formula I was creating would be successful. To me, it was inevitable.

From there, my confidence grew. My recipe for success included the secret sauce of self-development. Every day for years, I have continued to layer my learning—this aids in redirecting thoughts, fears and sabotage. Never stop learning.

The next critical ingredient is grit. Confidence grows through triumphs of struggle, so get super gritty and tap into your perseverance. It won't be easy, but if you want it, go after it. And lastly, have a purpose. I don't care what your purpose is; it must be meaningful to you to outweigh the fears that will arise.

I dare you to stop *wishing* for it and start working towards owning it.

Jess Callegaro was a former healthcare counsellor who now runs her online health coaching corporation and is a regional vice president with Arbonne.

Jess works with women globally with the main intention of helping them getting healthier from the inside out. Whether it's with her clients or on her social platforms she is always striving to encourage women to invest in their mindset to change their limiting beliefs and end their sabotaging behaviours. She's also known for her crazy and unconventional quick workouts and her straight shooter approach to self-care. When she's not coaching she's often chasing her son Cruz around the house or getting lost in the wilderness.

Facebook: @JessNadine
Instagram: @jess.nadine.c
Website: www.jessnadine.com

CONFIDENCE SECRET #13
Passion Over Fear
Karen Kobel

Picture it. East Islip, Long Island, New York. Good Ole Schoolhouse Road. Street hockey, running bases, front lawn dance performances, swing set shows, roller skating showcases and neighbours being family.

Always creating, always moving, always dancing, always bringing people together. The talent shows, the dance recitals, the countless hours of dance classes, and competitions were where I thrived and wanted to be throughout my childhood leading me to choose Dance as my university major.

I was in a very supportive environment, but also an environment filled with "what ifs" and fear.

I quickly learnt that the "what if" fear-based mentality wouldn't get me to the stage and spotlight. So, I changed my major within a month of being away at college from Dance education to Dance performance. I pushed my way through college in 3.5 years rather than 4 years because I met Mia Michaels. She taught me about passion and fire and following your heart and soul's whisper were much more rewarding than following your fear and someone else's fear.

I spent my first marriage safe and secure yet, my heart and soul yearned for a voice. I allowed someone else's fear to take me over. When I got shingles I didn't have a choice but to listen. I laid in my sick bed for a month and a half, with a numb face due to Ramsay Hunt Syndrome. I had no balance because I couldn't hear. I was being taken care of by my mother-in-law watching hockey and The Golden Girls realizing I was in the entirely wrong place. It was heartbreaking because she was wonderful. But I was living someone else's vision while jokes from my father-in-law about my saggy two-face played over and over again, unending from the time I woke to the time I went back to sleep.

I sat in the perfect dining room in a 1911 heritage house with pocket doors, a china cabinet, a glorious staircase, and all those beautiful things a house contains. Yet I was crying my eyes out, knowing this was the wrong place and the wrong time. I was about to break more hearts than one, but I was about to save my soul.

I packed my suitcase, headed to New York City, close to home, and finished certifications and adventures I hadn't completed. I listened to my heart and soul. I followed my path to reconnect to my passion: Dance. I embraced positivity over negativity —persistence over being complacent. I lived on couches until I could save enough money to get my own place independently. I left behind millions (of dollars) to find myself, to grow, to evolve, and to find happiness in what I knew was true to me.

Today I stand here as a successful business owner, still with a studio, a smaller studio on many accounts after a pandemic. But still, my dream of owning a studio for people to come to move, meditate, connect, congregate, collaborate, and build community and I can honestly tell you what got me here and my confidence secrets for you: POSITIVITY. PERSISTENCE and PASSION.

I find freedom and inspiration in movement, whether I am watching or moving. I have been given an opportunity to integrate my diverse training into my Pilates and dance classes.

Over the last few years, I have found movement to be some of the best healing for the mind, body and soul. I love sharing my experiences and discoveries with those interested in moving to heal and tapping into one's mind, body, and soul for healing.

Karen Kobel has a BFA in Dance Performance from East Carolina University. She has been dancing for the past 38 years, teaching for the past 25 years and performing for various artists such as Mia Michaels, Jay Norman, Marjon Van Grunsven, Tomi Galaska, Mary Carbonaro and Peter Grey Terhune. She has performed on the Regal Princess  and Crown Princess Cruise ships, Madora, many local artists, as well as producing Stand Up and Dance with proceeds going towards Living Positive Kenya, North Shore Women's Centre, and other local initiatives. She is a STOTT Certified Pilates instructor, Simonson Certified Dance instructor, and CI Training, Certified instructor.

After returning from Kenya and Uganda in November 2013, she realized the importance of tuning into one's life purpose. After teaching women with HIV Pilates/Dance/Strength Training and listening to their life stories, Karen recognized her life purpose: to inspire others, especially women, to find their own voice just as she had found hers after many years of fear. Karen shares her experiences with others in the hopes that it will help them believe that anything is possible, and everything is possible! We are only here for a short time: Live, Love, Inspire, and Move.

Kahlena Movement Studio has been open since 2017. It was a previous studio that Karen taught at from the day it opened 18 years ago. Karen grew Kahlena from being a Pilates studio to a movement studio offering Pilates, Yoga, Dance, parent and toddler as well as kids dance, meditation, workshops and more.

Karen at Kahlena Movement Studio loves to collaborate with other groups to create great experiences such as International Dance Day, Dancing outside Amica Seniors Residence, Ever Green Seniors Home and Lions Gate Hospital. The community really enjoys the High School Grad Parades, Kids Camps and events focused on wellness and mindfulness. Karen also puts together special events for many women like the International Women's Day events and Shop Local for Women Entrepreneurs. That's not all, she loves to support others with Wellness, Mindfulness, flash mobs, fundraisers, and offering studio rentals.

Facebook: @KahlenaMovement
Instagram: @kahlenamovement
Website: www.kahlena.com

CONFIDENCE SECRET #14
I am a Chameleon
Katerina Klimes

I was born in Prague, under the communist hammer. At the age of seven we took a holiday and escaped under the watchful eye of semi-automatics over the Yugoslavian border. We spent a few months in a true refugee camp, and a year and a half in refugee housing. We learned German and started anew. I saw my father after two years, when he was released by the communists. We got into Canada because my amazing Babi (Grandma) sponsored us in 1984: we started anew again. We spent the next few years being dirt poor, while my parents learned the language.

After losing my country, friends, language, house, wealth and my whole extended family, I then lost my own family as I knew it to divorce. My mother always said," Fake it until you make it", and so we did. My journey continued with several more great losses.

At the age of 30 I moved to Taiwan, away from everyone. It took great confidence in myself to start yet again. I needed a fresh place to renew myself, away from the past. I had to heal. With my first pregnancy, I had to look deep into my soul. I needed to make the world better and safer for my children. I started a cosmetics company in Taiwan because no one had what I wanted. I wanted to heal with real botanicals and magnesium. In a few years I had 800 clients while doing what my heart desired. I grew, I healed, and I managed to help others with love.

When we left Taiwan after 13 years, it took a lot of strength to give up community, friends and stability again. But again, I went and started anew and continued with Mila Earth. I was scared, nervous and terribly broke, but it was nothing because no one had a gun to my head, I had the freedom to say what I wanted, I could move and travel and I had the right to believe my own convictions. Freedom is a gift. True confidence is earned through courageous acts, by surviving real hardship, living becomes the only real choice.

I know I am damaged, but my scars grow with love and understanding for human suffering. My friends and clients always tell me how positive I am without knowing the whole sordid story. It is easy to be positive when you have bread in your tummy, wine in your fridge, a roof over your head and lovely children to take care of that are your own (that no one can take away). I am safe, I am loved, I am blessed: I live.

No one sees the refugee in me, they see a blond, a Canadian. I made it! I am a confident chameleon.

Katerina Klimes is the owner of Mila Earth Bodycare. It started as an organically grown project to make truly natural products available. Originally started in Taiwan because Katerina wanted the best for her friends and family. It grew to over 700 clients worldwide, just through referrals. Every product can be customized and used in a  variety of ways because quality and small batches are the true priority. We recycle all containers and believe in educating each new Mila Earth family member to buy local, create their own products, or buy from us.

Email: milaearthbodycare@gmail.com
Facebook: @Milaearthbodycare
Website: www.milaearth.com

CONFIDENCE SECRET #15
Financial Confidence
Kathryn Finn

When life changes unexpectedly, whether through the loss of a loved one, a torn marriage, dissolving the family business or an unforeseen illness, you may feel as though your world is pulled out from beneath your feet. Over the past 25 years as an Investment Advisor, I've become a safety net for many professionals when helping a family or individual get through difficult times.

I have worked with women in varying circumstances. From a stay-at-home mother of two, whose high school sweetheart never returned from a bike ride and left her with a mountain of debt. To a woman in her sixties who built up the courage to leave her unhappy marriage, having never made a financial decision in her life. I understand having economic confidence is not innate.

When my clients take on a new-found financial responsibility, either by choice or by consequence, I'm often asked, "Where do I begin?". These women have courageously committed themselves to learn a new language and a new way of thinking, the weight of their family's dreams and goals now resting on their shoulders. To dampen a seemingly daunting journey, I begin by guiding them through the following:

Become Empowered:
Decide what financial independence looks like for you. Is it able to pay your bills and save? Is it selling your business in eight years for ten million dollars?

Educate Yourself:
Have a financial plan and take the time to understand it. Having a sense of your financial position will give you peace of mind when you are in the driver seat.

Gather Your Team:
Surround yourself with professionals who will listen to and understand your needs. Your team will clarify your plan and hold you accountable for actions to attain your goals.

Witnessing my clients gain the confidence to become financially independent is incredible. It reaffirms why I chose this as my lifelong career.

Woman to woman, we've come a long way in tackling the social stigma of women and money, but we still have a journey ahead of us to control our financial well-being; gaining economic confidence is a significant part of that journey.

Kathryn Finn is sought out by individuals, and professionals alike, to advise them through life-altering events. Women make up the majority of Kathryn's clientele, and she thrives on empowering them to achieve financial confidence through her guidance and education.

LinkedIn: @kathrynfinn
Website: www.kathrynfinn.com

CONFIDENCE SECRET #16
Unlocking the Door to Presence
Kathy Bolton

The key to unlocking confidence has been the insight that, "My thoughts are the foundation on which my feelings come to life". This foundation is created either consciously or unconsciously by my state of awareness in each moment. Thoughts continually unfold in our minds and build the foundation of individual experiences.

I have to admit that confidence for me is like the ebb and flow of the ocean. Sometimes my sails are full of the wind, and I am on course, and then other times, I get lost in the expansive and uncharted ocean of life. When I am lost, doubting my abilities and questioning my capabilities, I remember I have the choice to bring in new thoughts and consciously build the foundation I choose. When my thoughts take me to a dark place of fear and negativity, they tell me I am not good enough or smart enough or kind enough; I take a deep breath and focus my attention on just being present and very still.

In this stillness, a key unlocks the invisible door to the perpetual now. This stillness quiets the ongoing dialogue in my head, and I can then hear a quieter voice. This soft voice is of my heart and soul, where I deeply connect to the sacredness of all life. As I become still, I enter into a presence where judgement falls away, and I know that I am who I am, and that is more than enough.

My true confidence resides in who I am, not what I am. As I strengthen my connection to stillness and presence, life transforms because I am not just reacting to my life or trying to figure it all out. I am engaging with life and creating it. As life's narrative unfolds, I know that all things are possible, and choice is ever-present in the next thought.

Kathy Bolton is an Entrepreneur, Fashion Designer and Wardrobe Coach. She always dreamed of a career in fashion design, realized when she found her niche. She empowers women to embrace the authentic expression of themselves through conscious fashion design and personalized wardrobe coaching. Confidence shines from the inside out, and  clothing is an expression of each woman's personalized style.

Kathy discovered many women were looking to elevate their expression of themselves through their wardrobe. She has created a program where she shares her in-depth knowledge and guides women to their personal style, resulting in the expression of inner confidence.

Kathy continues to evolve through ongoing personal development, continually fine-tuning her craft and partnering with like-minded individuals. Threshold Design Studio is her personal clothing brand created and consciously designed to empower and support women.

Email: thresholddesignstudiocanada@gmail.com
Facebook: @ThresholdDesignStudio
Website: www.thresholddesignstudio.com

CONFIDENCE SECRET #17
The Art of Gratitude and Appreciation
Kathy Fester

What does a confident person look like? How do you seat yourself in confidence in life? At the core of my being, the secret is how I show up in "Gratitude and Appreciation" with heart centred actions.

Living in your authentic genuine self and sharing value with others provides an opportunity to build and create a human connection on a foundational level. By performing this positivity creating action, you are then giving kindness to yourself and the receiver.

Gratitude is often a way of saying thank-you. It is the heart and soul of many of my colleagues, friends, and family. One of the ways of living a confident life is the giving of an authentic "Thank-you." Two powerful words when used together! By showing and sharing Gratitude with no ego attached, means not expecting anything in return. Gratitude is the emotion behind the prompting of the action of Appreciation.

Confidence is a feeling of self-assurance arising from one's Appreciation. Whether reaching out with a phone call, a gesture, a small token, a card, or a hug, Appreciation is a heart-centred way to create confidence in others and to show they matter.

Appreciation can be defined as the action step behind the emotion of Gratitude. How do you show up and share Appreciation with others? Appreciation in action is critical (and the secret) to round out the act of building confidence that what you have to offer the world matters. Now when you connect this with others, you become heart-centred, kindness-creating and invaluable to each other.

To sum up, the act of Human Connection is an aspect of a secret to confidence. Gratitude and Appreciation are other components. Share your beautiful self with everyone you meet using this secret and watch how it will change You and the World!

Kathy Fester is a loving, passionate, caring, and, most of all, a kind person. She is an author, speaker, relationship marketing strategist and a master teacher in the public-school system for over 30 years.

Kathy embraces the vision of life as a journey, and as such, the mission of Kathy's life is to change the world, one person at a time, through the act of kindness. Kathy's firm belief in the power of kindness sees her acting on promptings, having confidence, and being authentic with everything she does. She is always tweaking and learning.

Kathy has been with SendOutCards for several years. She has helped 100's of people develop their relationships with their clients/customer base through sending cards and creating campaigns for lasting referral business. After all, we do business with people we know, like and trust.

One-way Kathy is accomplishing the vision of world kindness is the G.A.S. (Gratitude and Appreciation Summit) event. As cofounder with Jeanette Martin, they have created a series of events to bring attention to how and why we choose Gratitude and Appreciation. How do you step on the G.A.S.

every day in your business, with others and most importantly, with yourself? How do you show Gratitude and Appreciation daily? Finding speakers, sponsors, venues worldwide, they are sharing this knowledge in unique and informative ways.

G.A.S. (www.gasummit.ca) and SendOutCards (www.sendoutcards.com/kathyfester) are her vehicles to meet people. Kathy helps develop their respective businesses and keeping in touch with clients and friends.

When not working, Kathy loves spending time being a mom, wife, sister, friend, aunt, daughter-in-law, plus loving life hard.

Email: kit@fester.ca
Facebook: @kathy.fester
LinkedIn: @kathyfester

"THERE WILL BE PEOPLE **WHO CHANGE YOU** & **PEOPLE YOU CHANGE.** *IMPACT WISELY.*"

~ DIANE ROLSTON

CONFIDENCE SECRET #18
Believe in Self
Laks Kutty

Confidence is a belief in oneself; if you believe you will do, you eventually succeed. I say 'eventually succeed' because you may fail, which is a great learning opportunity, learn, move on, and thrive.

I have always been curious. I was the first in the family to go to university. I started work in Information Technology (I.T.). Then I chose to pursue a Masters in I.T. While I was working on my Master of Sciences, I got married.

My philosophy has always been that you have a hand in your kismet (destiny). You always have a choice, and no matter how hard/easy life is, you can choose to have the last word.

I could have stayed in an unhappy marriage and adapted, but instead, I went through a divorce, quit my job, sold my belongings and moved to Canada. I initially stayed with my family, who held me back, so I moved out.

I believed in myself, my ability and had the confidence to go out into the world. It is all your own work and your own doing. A field will not grow food for you unless you put the work into it by ploughing, seeding, watering, and then harvesting the food—same in life. If you want more, do more, invest in yourself, believe in yourself, and the rewards will come. It may not be instantaneous; you may fail a few times, but success will come, and when it does, don't stop there. Make yourself another goal.

Women need to believe in other women, support other women, hold each other up because, for too long, we have been suppressed. Change the mindset, trust in your worth, believe that you can do it and have no doubt that you will succeed. Put the work in, ask for help and most importantly, don't listen to others who say you can't or that negative voice inside yourself; believe in YOU. Only YOU can make it work. I believe in you.

Laks Kutty is a confident woman of colour, an immigrant, a mother, a working professional and a business owner.

Laks is a first-generation Punjabi woman born to parents who moved to England from Punjab in the late 1960s. She immigrated to Canada in 2003, where she met her partner and had two children while building a new career. In 2008 she went to college and gained a Management Certificate in Human Resources.

After kids, she went to university in her 40's. She took on a Graduate Certificate in Executive Coaching while working full time. After graduating, she started her own business, Laks Kutty Coaching, which she runs while working full time and running a busy household.

Facebook: @lakskuttycoaching
Instagram: @LaksKuttyCoaching
LinkedIn: @laks-kutty-coaching

CONFIDENCE SECRET #19
Overcoming Barriers to Leadership
Linda Hunt

I have always considered myself to be a leader. Having spent 25 years in the public sector, corporate world and eventually as Executive Director of a national health charity, I led confidently. However, in 2009 at the age of 43, that ended. Ten years previously, I was diagnosed with a chronic neurological disease with no cure. And in 2009, I was forced to give up my one-hour highway commute for a shorter commute down the hall to my home office.

I learned that despite the barriers I faced, I could continue to be a leader in business and my community. The key to this realization was understanding that I still possessed the CONFIDENCE to be a leader.

The main barriers to leadership people face are:
- Attitudinal barriers
- Opportunity to participate
- Physical barriers
- Accommodations or assistance required.

The fundamental principles to overcoming these barriers are:
- Recognize a barrier for what it is
- Focus on what you CAN DO
- Provide solutions
- Focus on ABILITY, not a disability
- Hone Leadership skills
- Achieve goals
- There's a benefit to shared experiences

When advocating for yourself, be:
Resilient, Determined, Creative and Resourceful

Linda Hunt is an Award-Winning Accessibility Consultant, Speaker and Author. She is the CEO of Accessibility Solutions and an Advocate for all things related to accessibility.

Linda is the Treasurer of Citizens with Disabilities - Ontario and a long-standing volunteer in her community.

Linda first became a person with a disability in 2004. Since then, she has been an active and engaging speaker to groups on various accessibility topics.

Linda has more than 30 years of experience in senior management roles in the public, private and not-for-profit sectors. Prior to 2009, Linda held several leadership positions with the Provincial and Federal Governments, private companies and a National Health Charity both at the provincial and regional levels.

Based in Brantford, ON, Linda and her husband Greg have operated Grelin Apparel Graphics for over 30 years.

Email: linda@solutions4accessibility.com
LinkedIn: @lindahuntaccessibility
Website: www.solutions4accessibility.com

CONFIDENCE SECRET #20
Little Leaps to Confidence
Maria Conde

The last time you watched one of your favourite speakers on stage with hundreds of people watching, did you say to yourself, "I could never do that." Yet internally, you wonder and dream what it would be like to feel that exhilaration, to experience that level of confidence? Maybe your dream is not about speaking, but something else, something you don't feel confident enough to start.

Confidence is something that develops over time by taking action and doing the work. I have found that to improve confidence, you need to take the first step... and then another. I call these steps- little leaps! Using action and persistence to grow your confidence is one way to achieve significant success.

Far too many people give up when it gets hard; fear kicks in when they push and get out of their comfort zone.

It is also important to acknowledge all the small wins with every step you take. Celebrating small victories is often missed, and then we feel like we are not succeeding, so we stop taking action. Little leap, celebrate, little leap, celebrate is how you will naturally build your confidence and achieve your goals.

What is one little leap you can do today towards your goals?

Maria Conde is a best-selling author, host of the Leap to Freedom Show and CEO of Flourish & Freedom. She helps high achieving women create extraordinary lives and businesses for themselves that are rooted in the philosophies of freedom, purpose and prosperity. She believes in living life on your terms!

Maria is a certified health, money and life coach as well as a nutritionist. Before being a coach, she spent 30+ years in leadership as a CPA. She brings all this training and experience to her multi-faceted programs. Maria helps women transition from employee to entrepreneur and build a purpose-led business by clarifying their vision, strengthening their mindset and developing and executing a clear plan.

Maria is very much a multi-passionate entrepreneur who also has a health coaching membership for those that want to live a natural, healthy life.

Maria believes in and lives a life of purpose and freedom. When she is not serving her clients, she spends time with her daughter, playing tennis, philanthropy work and travel (to name just a few!)

Facebook: @mariacondecoaching
Instagram: @mariacondecoaching
Website: www.mariaconde.com

CONFIDENCE SECRET #21
Self-Esteem to Confidence and Back
Melanie ter Borg

When I quit my position as a biomedical researcher to start my own business, something happened I did not expect. My identity was no longer linked to what I did in the past. But instead with what I was doing now. And what I was doing was experiencing set-back after set-back in my entrepreneurial pursuits.

In the beginning, it seemed fine; I liked and believed in myself. Fail forward fast, right?! I was enthusiastic and motivated about my succession of businesses. However, by not practicing the profession I was good at and continually testing and stretching myself, my confidence plummeted. I was running on a diet of courage and endorphins, repeatedly hitting a wall of hot white failure. How could I get my mojo back?

In short, I felt more and more like I had nothing to contribute: I was worthless, and I brought no value to the table. My negative self-talk was screaming at me!

I dove into action, but herein lies the rub: do not conflate self-esteem with confidence. Each is different. Self-esteem is an internal belief that you are OK just the way you are, despite making mistakes. Self-confidence is an external feeling; it is trusting your ability to engage in the world successfully or adequately through the roles and tasks you perform.

My self-confidence success tips are:
- Eat nourishing foods and get that 30 minutes of daily exercise that works for you- the stamina of good health gives

you confidence, energy, and the ability to maintain good posture.

• Always acknowledge everyone in the room by saying hello and goodbye (or at least eye contact and a nod of recognition). You get what you give.

• Set yourself up for easy external confidence-boosting wins by volunteering for an organization that genuinely excites you and speaks to your values. Do not stay too long, though; COVID has taught us that women's unpaid labour should not be sustainable!

• My biggest tip, though, is to identify if you have a self-esteem issue or a self-confidence issue. Action can be a slippery slope, but "being" with self-esteem is a prophylactic for not losing your mojo in the first place! Seek the help you need when you need it.

Melanie ter Borg was a lab research technician and holds degrees in Cell Biology, Sustainability Management, and Women's Studies. She's taught, co-authored papers, and been involved in numerous start-ups in plant virology, stem cells, cancer, auto-immune disease, food sovereignty, and new technologies. She can be found living the dream sailing  her boat and helps people stay healthy, fit and entertained.

Email: melanie.ter.borg@gmail.com
LinkedIn: @melanieterborg
Website: www.melanieterborg.com

CONFIDENCE SECRET #22
The "YES" Word
Michelle Abraham

If I didn't have the confidence to step out of my comfort and continually expand that zone, I wouldn't have had the success I have had in life. I've lived a life where others have told me, "I'm so lucky," or I heard others say, "I wish I could do what you do." I don't think I am unique nor blessed more than others; in reality, my confidence stems from tragedy.

I experienced a life-altering event when I was 19 years old. I was having the summer of my life with my two best friends backpacking around Europe when my life changed. My friend Robyn and I were woken from our bed and taken to the hospital in Nice, France, where we learned our dear friend Cecilia was killed by a train that night. My heart broke, my world changed, and my perspective on life would never be the same.

I was blessed to learn you can't take anything for granted, life is short, and you don't have control over how long you have. I made a promise to my 19-year-old self. I will always say YES to Adventure, YES to new opportunities and experiences and YES to myself. I committed to living life on my terms and have FUN doing it.

By saying YES to those three things, I often land so far out of my comfort zone at times that, consequently, I have to dream bigger to get out of that zone now. Every time I have taken action towards a new YES, I have gained more and more confidence. I believe it has been connecting with others: building a community around me and collaboration, which are components of my confidence. Yet, saying YES is my ultimate SECRET to Confidence!

Michelle Abraham is a Speaker, Podcast Expert and Author of The Profitable Podcast. Michelle was voted #16 of the top 50 Moms in Podcasting by Podcast Magazine and Business from the Heart awarded her Entrepreneur of the year. Michelle is the Founder of Amplifyou. Kevin Harrington, the original shark on the hit T.V. show Shark Tank  says, "Amplifyou is North America's Top Podcast Management Company".

Michelle's team specializes in done for you podcast services for Entrepreneurs. They make, market, manage and monetize podcasts. Michelle and her team have launched and managed well over 142 podcasts in the last 18 months and manage over 55 shows weekly. Michelle is also the co-founder of The Canadian Podcast Network, and MyPodcastCoach.com Michelle has been mentoring and sharing her passion for podcasters since 2012! Michelle is so passionate about a freedom lifestyle that she lives off the grid on a lake and drives her kids to the school bus by boat, all while running a 100% online business.

Facebook: www.facebook.com/groups/ MyPodcastCoach
LinkedIn: @michelleeabraham
Website: www.mypodcastcoach.com/gifts

CONFIDENCE SECRET #23
You Deserve an Abundance of Confidence
Nicole Doumont

How would your life change if you had an ABUNDANCE of CONFIDENCE? Better relationships? A better career Opportunities? Improved happiness? So many women like you and I are struggling with low self-confidence every single day!

I believe there are eight reasons why:
1. Disapproving authority figures
2. Uninvolved/preoccupied caregivers
3. Authority figures in conflict/parents fighting
4. Bullying
5. Academic challenges
6. Trauma
7. Conflicting belief systems
8. Society and social media

Can you relate to any of these? I can relate! How? I have lived with depression for many years, and I've had to dig deep within myself to develop healthy habits to build my confidence over time so that I have the ability to live the life that I deserve. It hasn't been easy, but I know it can be done.

Structure breeds confidence; here is my list of how you can move forward and start building your self-confidence starting TODAY:

- Groom yourself and dress nicely
- Give to others
- Know your values and live them
- Knowledge is power, lean into learning

- Set goals and finish strong
- Volunteer for something you strongly believe in
- Start a daily practice of gratitude
- Exercise and eat right

Nicole Doumont, a co-founder of Elite Fitness Team Inc., has over 18 years of experience in the fitness industry. Nicole has coached thousands of people towards their ultimate health, fitness, and mindset goals!

Nicole struggles with depression, a prevalent mental health issue. She has dedicated her life to reducing and managing its impact on her life. While helping her clients do the same thing by working towards their TRUE POTENTIAL by transforming their health, fitness, and mindset!

Nicole coaches and helps her clients to increase their energy, increase their self-confidence, and transform their bodies through her online coaching programs! With the fitness and health industry being so overwhelming and confusing, Nicole coaches her clients one on one daily to ensure that their success is a top priority! While there aren't any quick fixes regarding your health, fitness, mindset, and overall well-being. Nicole's passion and unique coaching methods; aid, support, and guide her clients through their transformations!

Email: nmdoumont@gmail.com
Instagram: @nicoledoumont_elitefitnessteam
Website: www.elitefitnessteaminc.com

CONFIDENCE SECRET #24
A Conceptualization of Confidence
Paula Kent

There is a liminal space, a threshold of sorts between being confident and not being confident. In that space is the moment of transfer, where actions, thoughts, concepts and outcomes push us forward through the threshold into confidence - or pull us backwards into self-doubt and uncertainty. We can't see this space or touch it but oh, how we feel it. A bold sensation of surety enters our being as we move forward through the space, we feel light, yet a hint of the gloom of uncertainty remains in our mind. Throughout our life, we have stepped forward through the threshold a seemingly infinite number of times. We have arrived in the light of confidence over and over. Yet the gloom and darkness – our unique saboteur hovers just outside the space, dancing at the edges of our consciousness taunting us. Oh, the things that it says to hold us back, to stop us from stepping into our confidence. Mine can be nasty – "...you are too old," and "...you don't have the ability," or this powerful one "...what is the point, nothing you write is of value."

Far too often, we give that voice the power over us and meekly allow ourselves to be pulled back- when what we could do is to charge forward, leaving the darkness behind. To charge ahead is to embrace our self-doubt, push the fear aside, and ignore the voice of the saboteur. If we can push ourselves to go forward, we create our own terms; we make our own surety. By generating power for ourselves, we do not give up. We do not give in – we reduce the intensity of uncertainty and infuse ourselves instead with hope and passion.

When that saboteur calls out, *that* is the moment for bravery, courageous and fearless, committing to ourselves that we will not be pulled backwards. With bold courage, we will be steadfast and stare down the saboteur, turning our backs on the gloom.

Make a promise to yourself that you will harness your strength and reach forward to grab that confidence sitting in the light. Be resolute and face the discomfort, be daring and take the confidence you have earned. It is there – just reach for it.

Paula Kent has awoken the dormant writer within; she is currently writing her first book, Heroic Choices, The Inner Journey of Transformation. Due to be published in spring 2021. Paula is honoured to have the opportunity to participate again in the Dynamic Women® Secret Series. As a blogger, Paula publishes content weekly, which  explores the challenges women experience in modern society. And provides inspiration for all women to embrace their Rebelle Souls and create their most authentic lives.

Email: pjkent@telus.net
LinkedIn: @paulajkent
Website: www.rebellesoul.ca

CONFIDENCE SECRET #25
How to Make Your Confidence Roar
Robyn McTague

What I have learnt is that confidence comes from within. It sounds so simple, yet it's not always easy.

It can feel daunting putting yourself out in the world and risk being vulnerable or rejected. It takes courage. Society would have you believe that you will find the answers if you follow the current trend or thought leader. Instead, use this simple process to gain clarity and confidence. Dealing with breast cancer was my catalyst to go within and find my answers. It took commitment, practice and sitting in discomfort. Using these steps, you will build trust with yourself, be courageous and, in turn, confident.

The 5 C's are:
1. Create your sacred space by making it your own.
2. Connect to your truth and let go of intrusive thoughts.
3. Compassion for self as you feel your feelings.
4. Commit to reflective scheduled time, which builds stamina, endurance and capacity.
5. Celebrate your successes and have fun, with your inner genius cheering you on!

Practicing these steps will build inner trust. Trust is a by-product of being honest and in truth. We each have our own version of 'the truth' because of who we are. Determine what is true for you. I lied to myself about my true happiness and stayed in bad relationships, and did unfulfilling work. When I became honest with myself, I felt very uncomfortable. I learned to connect with my spirit, where I had a choice to be confident.

I tapped into my inner lion once I stopped lying. With courage, honesty and support, my confidence roared.

"You have plenty of courage, I am sure. All you need is <u>confidence</u> in yourself. There is no living thing that is not afraid when it faces danger. The true courage is in facing danger when you are afraid, and that kind of courage you have in plenty." The Wizard of Oz.

When you connect with your inner lion, you confidently step into your life of freedom, choice and joy.

Robyn McTague is a published author, a prolific writer and speaker, and the creator of A Life of Choice Coaching. She learned confidence by overcoming breast cancer, Hepatitis C, and other challenges.

Due to Robyn's experiences, she has a wealth of understanding and knowledge to help people on their healing journey in a safe, gentle, compassionate and practical way.

Her personalized system allows you to let go of the lies and embrace the courage of your own inner lion. Her areas of expertise include relationships, psychology, meditation, motivation and conflict resolution.

Email: robyn@alifeofchoice.ca
Facebook: @robynmct
LinkedIn: @robynmctague

CONFIDENCE SECRET #26
The Art of Playful Evolution
Rose Kapp (Roszay)

Evolution. Change. Re-Invention. You might not think these words refer to you and your business, but they do. The process doesn't have to be dreadful or difficult. It can be the result of play.

During my 35 years in the advertising and graphic design field, I became accustomed to the pace of change. In the '80s, I had to add computer graphics to my art practice because it didn't exist in my '70s art education. As an older designer, I recently decided not to compete for clients with the bright young things crowding the market. That meant making deliberate choices in my creative focus and still be marketable. Illustrative artwork was a natural shift.

My next change was not a conscious decision. It happened when I started an art challenge involving drawing for 100 days. Instead of my usual analytical renderings, I decided to let my pencil wander. What began as playful doodling transformed into decorative birds. By day 231, my first 'punny' caption appeared, and I was well on the way to my goofy Worry Birds' wry observations of life. They evolved in style and content in the over 1800 drawings created over the past five years. I was having fun.

This playful style infects my other works, namely house portraits. I "wonkify" the architecture and add details that reflect the spirit of the building. The whimsy shows, and clients continue to commission me to paint their homes. One recent homeowner claimed, "Oh, so sweet! Do I live there? I'm so lucky! I love our little abode and you gave it such character and life! I almost expect it to giggle!"

Change is going to happen. You will either make specific shifts in your business operations or make decisions based on events outside of your control. There's always a chance that you will go through a subtle evolution that will leave you surprised and delighted in the end. Wouldn't it be great if it happened through play?

Rose Kapp (Roszay) studied advertising art at the Alberta College of Art before moving to Vancouver. Recently, she has focused on her cartoons, commissions and gallery work. As an arts advocator, she hosts a group, Creative People Talking, an artist networking and support community on Facebook.

Email: roszay@shaw.ca
Facebook: @RoszayCanada
Website: www.rosekapp.com

CONFIDENCE SECRET #27
Want Confidence?
Focus on Your "End Game"
Shelly Lynn Hughes

Confidence is an intrinsic and purposeful state of being and entirely accepting of oneself and the inevitability that things will work out one way or another. When I think of confidence, I think of a calm assuredness of who I am and what I'm doing.

Confidence is contagious and magnetic and a massive source of success in personal and professional endeavours. It is the idea that if I focus on an end goal, that objective becomes more important than ensuring a 'perfect' path forward. If my focus remains steadfast, I will not be as worried about the process or approach to get there. A river will always find its way, even if it has to carve a new path through the rock. It's not worried about how it will get there; it *will* ultimately reach its objective.

Of course, being confident doesn't mean mistakes won't occur, or one must be perfect; if anything, it means the opposite. It's okay not to be perfect and find a new path forward while keeping your eye on what you ultimately want.

The confidence to fail allows me to pivot when something isn't working. If I make a mistake or a series of errors, or if something goes wrong. Keeping the end goal in mind and knowing that it's a good goal allows me to restructure, stay focused, and maintain my conviction. I continue to progress into the next stage and continue to work towards that same outcome.

Being confident in the end goal will lead to a new path and a way forward. We all have our paths and dreams, and very few routes are smooth and easy. Still, when I think back on the most incredible and memorable learning moments in my life, they all stemmed from going 'off-path'.   I encourage you that when your path deviates from the plan, know that it's a new opportunity to reach your goals in a new way!

Shelly Lynn Hughes is the founder of Fresh Magazine and a partner in Project Her Inc. and yoyomama.ca. She is currently writing a book titled pursuit:365, launching on International Women's Day – March 8, 2021. In addition to her work as a publisher and business owner, she has also developed an exclusive skincare label for a major  pharmacy and consulted for various magazines and health and beauty brands. Shelly loves to get her hands on an idea, make it a reality, and share it with the world—all while radiating the good vibes of a best girlfriend.

Email: shelly@freshmag.ca
Instagram: @fresh_mag
Website: www.freshmag.ca

CONFIDENCE SECRET #28
Being Confident While Being Different
Simer Grewal

Confidence starts by stepping out of your comfort zone. I stepped out of my comfort zone when, at the age of 20, I moved myself across the world from India to the United States to pursue my dreams.

Confidence isn't something one is born with; it is something that is within you. The more we put ourselves in situations outside the comfort zone, the more our confidence increases. My mom always encouraged me to follow my dreams and do things differently. She always used to say, "if you extend your comfort zone, you extend your confidence by extending your beliefs about what you're capable of doing." My personal belief is, "If you put your heart and mind to something, nothing is IMPOSSIBLE." We will stand out when doing things differently, which makes us, our business, and our products and services unique.

One needs to feel comfortable in your own skin and with what you do. No matter what colour, ethnicity, or business you are in, you will always find people who will criticize you regardless. Please don't give in to their criticism; instead, use that energy to fuel your desire and confidence. To be confident in what you do and who you are, one needs to understand who really is in charge of your emotions and actions.

To sum it all up, the confidence secrets I live my life by are:
- Extend your comfort zone to extend your confidence.
- Be persistent in what you believe in.

- Be confident while being different. You will always stand out by being different from the crowd.
- Take charge of your thoughts, emotions, actions and destiny to emerge as a Winner every single time.

Simer Grewal was born in India and moved to North America for further studies in 2005. Simer has an undergrad in Computer Science from India and an MBA from the United States. Following her MBA, Simer worked with a few Fortune 100 companies but wasn't happy, as just working wasn't enough. She had a deeper purpose. In India's '80s  and '90s, computer science for girls was not an important career choice compared to a doctor or educator. Defying all norms, she completed her education. She gained valuable experience, which empowered her to follow her dream of teaching kids, especially computer sciences, to girls.

Email: sgrewal@levelupkids.ca
Facebook: @levelupcloverdale
Website: https://centralsurrey.levelupkids.ca

CONFIDENCE SECRET #29
From Terrified to Confident
Stefani Chies

I've always had lots of confidence in the services I provide and the products I use. In the first year after I started my company, I generated many new referrals and leads via word of mouth. This success gave me even more confidence, and my business skyrocketed in the next couple of years.

Then I decided to start an online shop to share the products I was using. At this point, I hired my first business coach. My confidence nearly died when she told me the best way to market was video. SORRY, WHAT?! Video use had begun to get super popular and one of the best ways to market and be seen. It was the last thing I wanted to do. I was terrified.

She said, "Start with short two-three minute videos talking about one product".

I thought to myself, how am I possibly going to do this and be confident at the same time as being nervous and terrified?! Those limiting beliefs emerged; what if they don't like me? What if no one listens? What if no one buys? What if I suck? I was afraid of judgement.

Stepping out of my comfort zone, I knew it had to be done and did my first video. It was scary. However, after a few, I started to feel more comfortable. Fast forward a few years, I enjoy getting on video, and I'm super confident!

I learned to worry less about what others think and more about what I was sharing. I learned to be authentic on video as well as text.

That's my biggest tip to you. Do the uncomfortable, be you, and the confidence will grow and flourish.

Stefani Chies first started playing with makeup artistry in high school and was instantly fascinated with how you can change the way a person looks either entirely or by enhancing natural features. After high school, she attended the Blanche MacDonald Centre for Makeup Artistry.

After a few years of freelancing, she finally started her own company and, through that journey, has re-branded three times... yes, that's right. Doing the scary thing ended up helping her business evolve to where she wanted to be. She now offers beauty services and is partnered with various clean beauty companies and is also branching out to education for beauty professionals.

While being a busy mom of two, Stefani has a passion for helping others and finally discovered the best way for her to do it, through education for those in her industry. She is excited to help other beauty professionals grow their business and fill in the missing gaps from various training programs out there for all creative beauty services. The great part of this is, she can do it from home while raising her kids.

Email: hello@scobeautygrp.ca
Instagram: @scobeautygrp
Website: www.scobeautygrp.ca

CONFIDENCE SECRET #30
Surfing the Confidence Wave
Susan Davidson, P.Eng.

It's a tricky thing - confidence, particularly for women. Research shows women are expected to be "nice" before they are considered to be qualified. When things are going smoothly, confidence builds. But then life overwhelms with rough seas, and confidence sinks.

We need the right amount of confidence in order to thrive in our careers and be able to sell our services or products to others. How to get out of a confidence trough and start climbing up to the wave crest once more?

The first thing I look to is self-care. When I feel undervalued and overwhelmed, it is usually due to putting my own needs low on the list of priorities. So, ask yourself these questions:

- Have I been getting enough sleep lately?
- What about exercise, or just "being" in nature?
- When was the last time I did something just for pure enjoyment?

Secondly, examine your expectations regarding success. Failure is a vital part of success - statistics show that white male entrepreneurs endure failure at least 11 times in their careers. Implicit biases tell us that women should be perfect and never fail. If we never take risks, we lose the opportunities to learn from failures. By reaching out to others and sharing both negative and positive experiences, you can build a community of support to help you rise from the trough onto the crest of the confidence wave.

Susan Davidson, M.S., P.Eng. is a registered professional engineer in British Columbia and Nova Scotia, with 35 years of experience in the consulting industry. She has worked on projects throughout Canada and internationally.

Susan's areas of specialisation are coastal and ocean engineering. As engineers, we apply scientific principles to the solution of real-world, right-now problems. In this field, problems might include designing for shoreline erosion, adapting to climate change, estimating the effects of extreme storms on coastal and ocean structures, developing marine renewable energy sources, or assessing the environmental impacts of proposed coastal and marine projects.

Susan is the founder and owner of Sea Science Inc., a specialized marine consulting firm located in Vancouver, BC. Her favourite time to go to the beach is during a wind storm.

Email: shd@seasci.com
LinkedIn: @susan-davidson-ocean-engineer

CONFIDENCE SECRET #31
I Can Just Do It
Terryl McAlduff

How does one who is low in confidence, shy and quiet become a successful entrepreneur? I just did it.

When I was growing up in Calgary, my passion was to become a writer. Period. After high school, my shyness kept me from going to my preferred Journalism School, so I attended the hometown Journalism program at Southern Alberta Institute of Technology. Then in my second year, for some reason, somebody talked me into running for Communications Vice President on Student Council. After a lot of prodding, I said yes. I spent my second year being "publisher" of the weekly student Newspaper "Emery Weal" and the annual Yearbook. My quiet "Just do it" confidence started growing.

I graduated from college, spent a year selling advertising for a newspaper in Leduc, then I moved to Vancouver. My mother always warned me to not "strap a typewriter to my back," so I leapt at an opportunity while temping in the marketing department at the Bank of British Columbia to apply for and got a permanent job in their marketing department. My quiet can-do attitude helped me eventually become the Marketing Coordinator for Canada after Hong Kong Bank took them over.

Years later, with a downturn in the economy and banks struggling, my experience and can-do attitude led me to a job offer with the bank's advertising agency. Years later, as my family and career grew, I jumped on another opportunity to specialize in direct marketing (DM) within the agency. At that time, DM was a form of marketing that was just being recognized in Vancouver.

Then after the birth of my third child, I needed to balance my life. I knew there were very few direct marketing specialists in Vancouver who also had advertising experience. So, I put on my can-do hat and opened my own business, "McAlduff Direct – One-to-One Marketing Specialist" My first client was CBC.

My secret? Listen to the "I Can," ignore the "I Can't," and..."Just Do It."

Terryl McAlduff has been involved in Marketing and writing for over 40 years. As somebody diagnosed with Multiple Sclerosis and living with it since 1986, she uses her can do attitude every day as an active business owner, entrepreneur, and community volunteer. She is currently working on publishing a compilation of "I Can" stories of people living with MS.  "The Day my Life Changed" now has its own Facebook page for people to follow.

Email: tmcalduff@gmail.com
Facebook: @TDMYL

CONFIDENCE SECRET #32
Don't Worry,
We've Done This a Million Times
Wendy Breen

Buying and selling a home is an important process, and so is hiring the experts to help you. But just because a Realtor state they have experience doesn't mean they are the best. There is a need to ask many questions before choosing your Realtor to feel confident you are getting the best support.

Here are my top 10 questions to ask when choosing a Realtor and the reasons behind them:

1. How busy are you? Busy Realtors can be very popular and well known, but if they don't manage their time or have others supporting them, they may not communicate well or return calls when you expect them too.

2. Do you work with a team of Realtors? If yes, you may not get the Realtor you want. Most new Realtors are good because they typically have time to spend with you and will be very attentive and eager.

3. Do they have confident mentors that will help them?
Having a confident mentor will help guide new Realtors through uncertain situations. Even if you choose someone without the experience, they can tap into their mentor to make sure the process goes smoothly.

4. What are your Marketing Strategies? You'll want to ask to follow up questions: Where is my property being advertised? On your website and in the newspaper? What are your thoughts on open houses? What steps will you take to get my house ready for MLS?

5. Will you provide references? A Realtor should be more than willing to have you read testimonials or speak with past clients. These endorsements can give you the confidence that they have done a great job in the past and have happy clients.

6. What are the Top 3 things that separate you from your competitor? Most Realtors will not hesitate to respond to this. You will get a variety of answers; look for what is important to you. Look for integrity, honesty, trustworthiness, assertiveness, a great negotiator, hard-working and an excellent communicator.

7. What is your commission? An important question. Everyone wants a deal, but you also get what you pay for. A Realtor who cuts commission because another Realtor does may not work as hard for you or be as good a negotiator with a lower commission. Good Realtors will not reduce commission rates but will always try to negotiate the BEST price and conditions for YOU.

8. Can you help with other Professionals? A Realtor has a select group of professionals they work with and trust, including lawyers, home inspectors, mortgage brokers, licenced contractors and tradespeople. You can get excellent referrals, which saves you time.

9. Do you offer a Guarantee? Reputable Realtors will release clients from contracts if personalities clash or if working together is ineffective in maintaining their reputation.

10. Do you have any questions, or do you have something more to add? The Realtor may have other things they need to go over with you; give them the opportunity—Realtors interview clients simultaneously when clients are interviewing Realtors.

Make your decision based on what answers are important to you, not just the commission they charge. Always look at the whole picture.

Wendy Breen was a stay at home Mom until she decided she wanted a career that allowed her to still be there for her two children. Wendy started her schooling In Real Estate in the summer of 1998 and passed her three courses by Jan. 1999. Since then, she has helped her clients buy and sell properties and make their dreams come true. Wendy prides  herself on being honest, having integrity, and sharing the knowledge she has gained from her life experiences with her clients'. "I love to Help People Find Their Dream Homes, not a Money Pit!"

Email: wendybreen@sympatico.ca
Facebook: @wendybreensellshomes
Website: www.wendybreen.com

The Following Pages Contain
BONUS MATERIAL
from me & an extra Confidence Secret from my daughter!

CONFIDENCE SECRET #33
The Right Mindset to Be Confident
Bailey Rolston

It all began when I met my neighbour Alaina. I was selling popsicles when Alaina came to get one. She didn't just want to have a popsicle. She also wanted to be my friend. We started playing together, playing family with stuffed animals, riding bikes and making up songs and dances. Then we became friends. Mom says that kids become friends much faster than adults, and I think it's because we start playing together right away.

One day Alaina and I were drawing. When she looked at my finished drawing, she said, "Why can't I draw like you? You're really good at it, and I'm not." I replied to her, "You're good at other things like dancing, being outgoing and cartwheels." I offered to teach her how to draw better, and she agreed.

To teach her, I started thinking about what she likes. For example, she likes owls, so I chose an owl picture for us to draw. Before she came over, I figured out how to draw it myself. Then when she was with me, I showed her how to draw it step by step. Sometimes when she was drawing, I told her she did a good job and encouraged her, so she believed in herself. Over time and with my help, Alaina got better at drawing, and her confidence grew.

She became more confident with my encouragement, my teaching and by practicing. But the cool thing is I also became more confident in my ability to draw and my leadership. Part of my growth came because when she arrived at my house, her smile was small, but her smile was twice the size when she left. I saw how we both improved, and that made me feel proud.

Alaina and I have to keep remembering to choose a growth mindset. At school, I learned that a growth mindset is where you believe in yourself, and feel you can learn new things. A fixed mindset is where you don't believe in yourself and that you can't grow. I kind of think about it like a mountain that you are either going up or going down in confidence by choosing to have a growth mindset or not.

You can also build up your confidence by choosing a growth mindset. Here are my tips: Believe in yourself, or have others who do, learn from your mistakes, keep practicing and of course, have fun doing it!

Bailey Rolston is nine years old. She lives with her Mom, Dad, brother Bodhi and her cat Kali in North Vancouver, Canada. Since she was younger, she has enjoyed coming up with many business ideas to make money, like selling popsicles, paintings, and many other items. One of her favourite activities is creating art, usually with animals or  cartoons. She loves playing with friends, writing stories and doing tricks on the monkey bars. She wants to use her confidence to learn new languages.

When she grows up, she wants to be so many things; a veterinarian, a horticulturist, an explorer in New Zealand finding animals, a dessert baker, an artist, an actor and a wildlife photographer. Her hope for the future is that wildlife will be protected, and there won't be as many endangered animals.

To reach Bailey, contact her Mom at
diane@dianerolston.com.

"HAVE THE **COURAGE** TO STEP INTO THE **SUCCESS** YOU HAVE ALWAYS WANTED"

~ DIANE ROLSTON

Stop the Doubt from Killing Your Dreams
Diane Rolston

Wouldn't it be great if there really was such thing as an *'easy'* button? A whole lot more people would be following their dreams: like running your own business, trying something new and making a transition your soul tells you is right. But going after your dreams can be a scary thing. Your confidence must be high and if not, these questions will repeat in your head...

- Will this work?
- Should I just get a 9-5?
- Will I fail?
- Is this the right decision?
- What will other people think?

Feeling that fear or lack of confidence can mean you care about your success. But the bigger problem, one that I would call the #1 Killer of Dreams, is self-doubt. Self-doubt is slightly different, and manifests in subtle ways that slowly push you to sabotage yourself out of going for what you want. There have been plenty of times when I came close to giving up, and so I came up with an easy way to stop self-doubt in its tracks. Think of it like the ABCs – with no 'D'= Doubt!

A – Action: Do one small achievable action that will get you closer to your goal and those great ideas. By acting you'll feel the progress and build your confidence.

B – Brag: Know what you're good at and the value you offer so when you go into talks with others about your choices, your offers or anything regarding an exchange of money or a reward you know your worth and will ask for it.

C – Coaching: Having the support of your coach will give you the confidence to do things, will keep you accountable and will cheer you on (or kick your butt) towards what you really want helping you increase your money, progress and time!

Let's take a look at how self-doubt manifests and how the ABCs could apply to the three most common concerns when going for your goals: money, progress, and time!

How Self-doubt affects your Money: You lose money when you're not going for those clients, that promotion or that big project. You cave when you wanted to ask for the bigger sale. You take lower rates for your services and you constantly undervalue yourself reducing your profit.

A – Action: Ask previous clients, employers or even friends about what you had done for them and the value you offer. By getting testimonials you're results will speak for you and build your confidence.

B – Brag: Create your own list of the top 10 results people get by working with you or from you helping them. Then create another list of all of your skills and talents. When you read these lists over and over again you will start to believe the truth of how great you are and your confidence will grow. If you own a business make sure it's on your promotional material and website.

C – Coaching: Your coach will empower you to feel confident to ask for what you're worth by getting to the heart of why you devalue yourself. Then they'll hold you accountability when you go into meetings, so you don't decrease what you're worth. **Here is my coaching question for you to think about:** What is it costing me to not receive what I'm worth?

How Self-doubt affects your Progress: You don't follow-up with others you feel are above you or you're intimidated by and end up missing out on networking, friendships and even love opportunities. You don't do things that others haven't done in case you fail, so you end up not standing out or getting ahead. You don't put new products or

services into play or take a chance on your latest great idea so you stay in the same place. No process means limited success.

A – Action: Make a list of people who you'd like to get to know or do business with. Then pick a day, write it in your calendar and contact them. All it needs to be is a quick... "Hey, I would love to get together this weekend!" or "Hello, can we make a Zoom appointment to connect?"

B – Brag: Speak up about your great ideas. Whether for your business, a community group or your family, being heard builds confidence especially when they pick your idea. Share your progress on social media and with friends so they can mirror back to you how well you've done.

C – Coaching: Having a coach to bounce ideas off of can help to get you clear about which ones you want to pursue and which ones you want to put on the back burner. Then by creating a plan together you'll have a clear picture of where you are going and by committing to action you will make progress.
Here is my coaching question for you to think about: Where do I get held back?

How Self-doubt affects your Time: You're spreading yourself too thin and being everything to everyone and end up being too busy. By lacking the confidence to say "no" to others or speak up for yourself it's costing you time to work on things that matter most and time to be with those you love the most.

A – Action: Make a list of all the things you're doing in every area of life. Then make a list of all the things you'd love to do if you had more hours in the day. Take one thing off your current to do list and instead replace it with something you'd love to do. Then make sure you do it – even for just five minutes.
B – Brag: Look at your list of responsibilities and figure which ones are not worth your energy and time anymore by asking

yourself: Do I love this activity? Do I need it? Do I want it? If the answer is no to all three – cut it out! If the answer is no to one or more, really think about if you can do it less, delegate it or just stop doing it.

C – Coaching: Your coach can help you to look at your priorities, and what you're missing out on. Then you can work together to choose where to spend your time and how to be more focused and efficient with it.

Here is my coaching question for you to think about that is important for your happiness:

What do I want to say, "yes" to in my life? For example, vacations, exercise, a dance class, date nights etc.

Now you have the ABCs you can apply when you have doubt. I really hope you will implement these ideas as I know they work.

Now, what about those five pesky questions? I haven't forgotten about them. When you hear…

· Will this work? Remember that the only way you'll know this answer is if you get into action on it.

· Do I really have what it takes? You just might! Every skill, every talent and every success can be applied to this new goal. If you say no before you have even started, there's someone else who will take the chance!

· Will I fail? You 100% will if you don't even try.

· Is this the right decision? Every decision and every step, even if it's wrong, gives you clarity towards the "right" decision for you.

· What will other people think? When you are confident, what other people think is less important to you, and you learn to stay focused on what you desire.

Want some support around applying the ABCs to go after your goals and make your dreams a reality, without the 'D' = Doubt? Just reach out to me.

"LEARNING
IS **FUEL** FOR
MOTIVATION."
~ DIANE ROLSTON

7 Ways to Keep Going During a Chaotic Time
Diane Rolston

If you feel that life's a bit crazy for you right now, you're not alone. At one point or another in your life (and probably multiple times), you will feel overwhelmed, out of control and unable to deal with the stress of it all. There has been so much panic around Covid-19, and it's starting to impact all areas of our lives negatively.

I get it. It's hard not to feel the stress when major newspapers like the New York Times print quotes like, "This week, it's all gone to hell!" Granted, it's been a very tough time, but this negativity is not what we should be feeding our minds. With every announcement documenting a rise in cases, our doom and gloom feelings also increase. And even on social media, we're inundated with virus stats, presumptions, and unsubstantiated claims. People are panic buying and hoarding unnecessarily, and it's taking food and supplies away from our most vulnerable. Yes, it's all overwhelming.

To help balance the chaos, I'm going to share the seven ways to keep your business and your life on track, both during a pandemic or any time you are feeling overwhelmed. You will have tools and strategies to get the most out of this time that we're in and any future stressful time.

1. Don't panic. Change perspective

We have to change our perspective and tap into how we're feeling right now. Even if you're not panicking, you need to tap into how you're feeling. If it's not a perspective that supports you, helps you, or keeps you in the right frame of mind, you need to pivot. Change it to a new perspective.
- What's your new perspective?
- What are you going to choose going forward?

- What emotion do you want to feel?
- What emotion is your current perspective eliciting?
- Ask yourself what your current perspective of the situation is?

Try on a bunch of perspectives, and you get to choose which one you want to move forward with.

For example, instead of thinking to yourself, "I'm being restricted! I have to stay in my home. I have to isolate, and I don't like this." How could you change your perspective? You could say, "I'm going to the cottage with my family, and we're going to play games, have fun, chill out, relax, and sleep in!" Doesn't that already sound much nicer?

2. Don't go out. Go inward

Don't look to outward things to bring you calm and to make you feel good. Going out to concerts, bars, restaurants, and even binge-watching TV are not going to serve you right now. Instead, go inward into yourself and reflect on what you need right now.

Do you need meditation? Prayer? Sleep? Reading? What about a course you've meant to do? Maybe you want to spend time with yourself. Look inward to see what you need because that's where a place of alignment will come from; your inner strength. Alignment what's going to support you when you move forward in life.

3. Don't grumble, Show gratitude

Grumbling doesn't serve anyone. We all know those people who complain about the weather today and something else tomorrow. All this attitude does is welcome more grumbling, more negativity, and more stress into your life. You are doing yourself a disservice by focusing on the negatives.

Instead, show gratitude. Here are some examples:
- Be grateful that you have electricity.
- Be grateful that you have food.
- Be grateful that you have clean air.
- Be grateful you're at home safe with your family.
- Be grateful for this extra "free" time granted to you.
- Be grateful that you're safe.
- Be grateful for all things in life, big and small.

4. Don't focus on symptoms. Focus on systems

You might be listening to the news and then notice you have a little sniffle. Maybe you feel a bit tired or warm. You're focusing too much on the possibility of those symptoms, when in fact, you should be focusing on your systems.

By systems, I mean positive habits. What habits in your life do you want to change? What things in your business aren't going well? Focus on creating systems to change your habits and routines?

Do you need a system for your taxes? A system for your health? A system for eating better? A system for getting more clients? A system for your social media?

Now's the time to create those new practices and lock them in. Systems make the world and life business rules so much better. Focus on these systems and stop focusing on the symptoms.

Yes, you need to self-monitor. Yes, you need to check-in on yourself and your family. But once you've checked in, move on, move on to something else, something that's going to help you when we come out of this time.

5. Don't lose your cool. Love on others

Don't freak out on other people. Don't be rude online. Don't be the hoarder at the grocery store. Don't be snippy with people. Instead, focus on the love for your friends, family, and even strangers. Now is the time to show kindness. Now is the time to love on people and do things to show you care. Write some cards, call a friend, have a zoom date, or do something that shows your love for others. One thing that I'm doing with my clients is I'm reaching out to them. And I'm checking in with them.

6. Don't suffer. Ask how you can serve

Don't sit there and put yourself into this place of suffering. Don't just sit at home and not use this time wisely. Instead, turn it around and ask, "How can I serve?" Put that negative energy of suffering into action.

How can you serve others right now? Do your neighbours need you to grab groceries for them? Are there people online who need your services?

I like holding events, masterminds, and training. Many of them were live in-person because there is so much community and connection built when we meet face to face. I'm having to adapt and redirect those in-person events online with video conferencing systems like Zoom. The beauty is that I get to work with so many more people; I am no longer restricted by location. The online community's diversity has allowed me to see and respond differently to how I serve others.

7. Don't be concerned. Get creative

Stop being concerned about every single thing that's happening. Watch the news, get your information and move on. Put your energy into being creative. Are you going to get creative in how you cook, in quilting, or photography? Could you turn something you usually do in-person into an online course?

For example, I got creative when I had to cancel a live event in Ontario. I moved it to an online platform and opened it up to the world so more people could be a part of it. I gifted it to everyone! Why not? By bringing the community together, positive energy gathers and generates; stress, pain and negativity diminish.

Looking back, how many of these seven things have you already implemented in your life or business? Which one(s) will you incorporate and move forward? Even if you can only pick one right now, imagine how much better would your life be?

"MEASURE YOUR LIFE BY SATISFACTION! ~~NOT SUCCESS~~."

~ DIANE ROLSTON

One Final Message

Congratulations!

You did it! You now know more than 34 stories and secrets to confidence. You should be proud of yourself! You have invested in yourself with your personal development and you will also grow professionally.

My mission with this book is twofold:
1. 1st to bring you a story a week from women you can relate to, be inspired by and connect with.
2. 2nd to bring to life the dream of many women to write a book.

I trust this book will motivate, inspire and empower thousands of women and then ripple out to those around you to impact tens of thousands with the confidence secrets.

My wish for you is that you…

"HAVE THE COURAGE TO STEP INTO THE CONFIDENCE YOU HAVE ALWAYS WANTED."

By following the simple confidence secrets in this book, you can start to feel the reality of the confidence you have dreamt of.

One step, each day to confidence.
You got this Dynamic Woman!
Mwah! Diane

YOU ARE A DYNAMIC WOMAN AND A TOP ACHIEVER!

SPECIAL <u>FREE</u> BONUS <u>GIFT</u> FOR YOU!

To help you achieve more success, there are free bonus resources for you at:

www.FreeGiftFromDiane.com

"WHO YOU ARE
MATTERS
MORE THAN
WHAT YOU DO."
~ DIANE ROLSTON

It's now your turn to
Be Confident!

Made in the USA
Monee, IL
09 December 2020

51909736R00069